Beautiful One

A Walk in Deeper Intimacy
With the One Who Created Us

Beautiful
One

BENI JOHNSON, HEIDI BAKER, SUE AHN, WINNIE BANOVA,
DEANNE CLARK, SHERI HESS, ANNE STOCK, NINA MYERS

EDITED BY SHAE COOKE

DESTINY IMAGE₍ₐ₎ PUBLISHERS, INC.
P.O. Box 310, Shippensburg, PA 17257-0310

"Speaking to the Purposes of God for This Generation and for the Generations to Come."

This book and all other Destiny Image, Revival Press, MercyPlace, Fresh Bread, Destiny Image Fiction, and Treasure House books are available at Christian bookstores and distributors worldwide.

For a U.S. bookstore nearest you, call 1-800-722-6774
For more information on foreign distributors, call 717-532-3040.
Reach us on the Internet: www.destinyimage.com.

ISBN 13 TP: 978-0-7684-3249-7
ISBN 13 HC: 978-0-7684-3438-5
ISBN 13 LP: 978-0-7684-3439-2
ISBN 13 Ebook: 978-0-7684-9120-3

For Worldwide Distribution, Printed in the U.S.A.
2 3 4 5 6 7 8 9 10 11 / 13 12

My lover spoke and said to me,
"Arise, my darling,
my beautiful one, and come with me.
See! The winter is past;
the rains are over and gone.
Flowers appear on the earth;
the season of singing has come,
the cooing of doves is heard in our land.
The fig tree forms its early fruit;
the blossoming vines spread their fragrance.
Arise, come, my darling;
my beautiful one, come with me"
(Song of Solomon 2:10-13 NIV).

CONTENTS

INTRODUCTION

by Shae Cooke

Beautiful One is so divinely inspired. At times I could scarcely write, the anointing on the Beautiful One Conference speakers' messages was *that* strong. Glory to God!

As I mined the depths of the Father's heart through these incredible women of God—Beni, Heidi, Sue, Winnie, DeAnne, Sheri, Anne, and Nina—I was heart-soaked by a sense of just how much Abba Daddy God desires His children, His daughters especially, to know of His vast love and heart for them. Women today, more than ever, are feeling stressed and excessively burdened, increasingly so in today's economic, social, and moral climate, which can cause us to lose hope and give up. Many of us cannot see God's eyes anymore. We have lost focus in the busyness of our lives. The enemy would like nothing more than to weigh us down further with His lies that we are not able, capable, or even worthy of God's blessings. He has caused a number of women to lose sight of their identity in Christ, of their first love, of who they are as beloved, adopted daughters. As a result, some of us have loosened our grasp on God's promises for our lives, settling in for less than God's best.

It is more important now than ever before that we realize that our hope is not just a future one, but a *present* reality, a lavish grace that we can hold today, walk in, cherish, and expect, even through tumultuous times. This, as you will see through the challenges and experiences of these women, comes about by being firmly planted in the Father's love, and by shedding the impoverished or religious mindsets that say, "Good won't ever happen to me," or "That's not the way God works!"

This book was birthed as a result of the August 2009 Beautiful One Women's Conference hosted by Global Awakening Ministries, Christ Community Church in Camp Hill, Pennsylvania, and Life Center Ministries International in Harrisburg, Pennsylvania. It comprises the core of the messages of its speakers—some of whom even expanded their message. Our prayers are that *Beautiful One* will not only richly bless you, but also the men in your life, as they come to a deeper understanding of the workings of a woman's heart and its true longings.

Beautiful One is unique in its refreshment for young and old alike, with a conversationally breezy, joyful, and humorous atmosphere; it is passionate, candid, and conversational in its approach. Here, world-class ministry leaders let their hair down for a meeting of like hearts, minds, and hunger for God, a melting pot of emotions and insights that will stir every aching heart toward Jesus. Read on, and get caught up in God's extravagant plan for your life!

Part I

In the Eye
of the
Beholder

*Like an apple tree among the trees of the forest
is my lover among the young men. I delight to sit in his shade,
and his fruit is sweet to my taste. He has taken me to the banquet hall,
and his banner over me is love. Strengthen me with raisins,
refresh me with apples, for I am faint with love*
(Song of Solomon 2:3-5 NIV).

Most little girls love sparkly, shimmery things, and the penchant for the glimmer usually follows us into womanhood. This attraction to light, and the desire to flaunt it, is how God made us—to shine! We shine beauty when the light of God's glory is upon us, when we wear forgiveness like a crown and are willing to emerge from the ash heap of misery, sorrow, destruction, and defeat into the miracle of the Cross, the lavishness of love's banquet hall and the spirit of adoption whereby we can cry out, "Abba!"

No wonder we crave such light in the contrasting gloom of darkness. When darkness overshadows, when the word of the Lord is rare, when everything seems contrary to how God tells us things should be, when we are feeling miserable, even ugly inside, we cry out in desperation, "Show me Your glory!" But guess what? God points to you and says, "Honey, arise and shine because *you* are My glory! All along I've been adorning you to shine in dark places!"

Though you may not see yourself as Abba's glory, our "beauty" experts, Heidi, Beni, and Winnie, in the following chapters, will challenge you to see yourself as the apple of His eye, His precious jewel of a daughter—loved, adored, and cherished beyond imagination—so that you can move into a whole, new, lavish *now*. Even if you are a mess, God can use you for His glory!

Their own transparent journeys into His heart will help you to see Him connecting the dots of His passion as He ambushes you with His love. Their experiences will help you feel Him syncing His heart with yours and encourage you to see Him on the other side of your cocoon, toiling to help you break through all that keeps you anxious and freeing you to soar into the realm of "I'm so full."

Chapter 1

PRAISE OF HIS GLORY AND
SEALED WITH A KISS

by *Heidi Baker*

Arise, shine; for your light has come!
And the glory of the Lord is risen upon you.
For behold, the darkness shall cover the earth,
and deep darkness the people; but the Lord will arise over you,
and His glory will be seen upon you (Isaiah 60:1-2).

Do you desire freedom? You are a daughter of the Most High God. In Him you are chosen, having been predestined according to the plan of Him who works out everything in conformity with His purpose, the purpose of His will, that we who were the first to hope in Christ might be to the praise of His glory.

Blessed be the God and Father of our Lord Jesus Christ, who has blessed us with every spiritual blessing in the heavenly places in Christ, just as He chose us in Him before the foundation of the world, that we would be holy and without blame before Him in love, having predestined us to adoption as sons by Jesus Christ to Himself, according to the good pleasure of His will, to the praise of the glory of His grace, by which He made us accepted in the Beloved (Ephesians 1:3-6).

Father is looking at you and thinking, "Wow! Look at her!" You are for the praise of His glory. If you have children, you love it when they do well, right? You don't say, "Why didn't you do better?" Father is thrilled when you offer Him your life, even if it is pitiful.

Know Whose You Are

Mozambicans hate dogs, especially big ones—more specifically, our two big, black labs, which are totally not trained except when there is food, then they are quick to "sit" on command.

On Sunday nights I host parties because we love get-togethers. We invite the same eight children, and they invite others, and it becomes a huge slumber party. Many come because they know there is a spirit of adoption on them; they walk in as if they own the place...and they do!

When the children arrive, the ones who have a spirit of adoption are quick to tell the dogs, "Sit!" It is the only word most can say in English. (The dogs speak Portuguese, but hey.) The first-timers, on the other hand, freak out around the dogs.

Now I'm not calling my puppies demons, but for the sake of this teaching, in the same way, if you have an orphan spirit, you are likely to cower and run off because you do not know that demons are subject to you.

> *Demons simply cannot stand it*
> *when you know to whom you belong.*

If you have a spirit of adoption and demons are around, you can command them, "Go!" and they will leave because you and they know that Papa Daddy God, who is huge, is standing by His adopted child! Demons simply cannot stand it when you know to whom you belong. Papa stands behind you, and you think it is you, and He's thinking, "Praising My glory, baby!" He loves it when you know whose you are.

You Go, Girl!

My children love to draw and scribble, and I treat every drawing, even a line, as a masterpiece, featuring their artwork on the refrigerator.

"It's beautiful!" I say, and down comes the old, and up goes the new. All our photos are also on there, but I have to move them around often to accommodate everything. The children love it and smile in their sense of belonging. In the same way, even if your attempt is a big scribble, Papa looks at it and says, "Wow, you are an artist!" and sticks it on His fridge in Heaven. "Look at that! It's amazing!"

This is how the Father reacts to His children. He does not expect us to do something before we are able. If you are a mother, you can relate; you don't give your children things to do that they cannot; rather, you bless them and encourage them on their way, as God does. Our Father is totally in love with us and is cheering us on, "You go, you go, girl!" He is delighted in our loving Him, our effort to love, our desire to love, and our heart that opens to love Him. He likes it! I like Him! We are included. You were included in Christ when you heard the Truth, the Gospel of your salvation, having believed that you are a child of God.

You can believe you are an orphan and stay that way, or you can believe that you are a child of Papa Daddy God and be transformed and move into a whole new realm in your life where you speak and Daddy backs you up because your heart is aligned with the Son, Christ Jesus.

> *You can believe you are an orphan and stay that way, or you can believe that you are a child of Papa Daddy God.*

S.W.A.K.

In Him also we have obtained an inheritance, being predestined according to the purpose of Him who works all things according to the counsel of His will, that we who first trusted in Christ should be to the praise of His glory. In Him you also trusted, after you heard the word of truth, the gospel of your salvation; in whom also, having believed, you were sealed with the Holy Spirit of promise, who is the guarantee of our inheritance until the redemption of the purchased possession, to the praise of His glory (Ephesians 1:11-14).

God has marked you with a seal. When He meets you with the spirit of adoption—when you say, "Yes" to your Daddy, when you say, "Yes" to Christ Jesus—He comes with a seal, with a fire branding, and brands you. Like a burning on your soul, His name is on you: *"They shall see His face, and His name shall be on their foreheads"* (Rev. 22:4). Sssss...you can feel Jesus branded there. Everywhere you go,

Jesus is evident. The burning bush travels with you into Target, Costco, where-ev-er! Isn't it amazing that (unless you wear a burka) you can cover every part of your body, but usually the face is left exposed? It is hard to cover a forehead seal! God sealed you, called you, destined you to carry His glory. He destined you to be a woman who knows who she is, a lover of an Almighty God, sealed by the Holy Spirit, adopted by the Father. You who believe are marked. He knows whose you are by the seal of the promised Holy Spirit who is a guarantee, a deposit guaranteeing your inheritance until the redemption of those who are God's possession. Are you? Are you God's possession? Yes? Then just give it all up for God. You are His possession! He is yours! Yeah!

I recall a time when I was praying for the Church to feed the poor and to see the broken and dying come to know the Living God. The Church was asleep, and I was broken over it.

"God, what are You going to do? Shake them or what?"

Do you know what He did? He kissed them. I watched as the Lord Jesus kissed the foreheads of His people and awakened them. "I will wake them with a kiss, a kiss!" He said, "I will awaken them with intimacy, and they will become alive in love, alive because they are in love."

FREEDOM TO GIVE, FREEDOM TO RECEIVE

Do you know why Jesus was free? Because He knew who He was. Son of God Most High. Loved by the Father. Jesus was free to leave Heaven and to be born in a dirty manger, to carry radical love and suffer and die because He knew who He was. He was free. Free to give Himself away, and that is what He did. He said, *"Now come and follow Me."* (See Matthew 4:19; 16:24; 19:21; Mark 1:17; 8:34; Luke 9:23; John 12:26.) No identity crisis. He knew exactly who He was, who He is, and who He will be forever and ever and ever. Christ Jesus just gave

Himself away that we would know that we too are adopted into the Father's house, that we too are able to marry the Bridegroom King, and be free to give away and receive.

You Can Never Be Too Rascally

One of my rascally sons, a youth I picked up off the street in rags, was angry, demonized, bitter, and furious. When I brought him home, he stole everything he could get his hands on and then ran away. This became a cycle. I'd find him and bring him home; he'd steal and take off again. He also had an abusive bent and assaulted people, but I never stopped telling him how amazing he was, how I believed in him as my son. One day I got a call that he'd tried to strangle one of our missionaries. "You know, son, that's not good. You really can't go around strangling missionaries. You are not an orphan; you don't need to strangle anyone for any reason."

> *You know, son, that's not good. You really can't go around strangling missionaries.*

"I know, I know," he'd say. We kept on loving him, and he'd mess up again and again until finally we were told by the powers that be that he could no longer stay in our home. So I built the young man a house, and do you know what he did? He filled it with orphans. Although he had a good heart, try as he did, he would mess up because he did not understand the spirit of adoption.

One day while conducting an outside meeting (Georgian and Winnie Banov were with us), a "religious," resentful mob showed up. It was a time in their religion when they could not eat, so they were quite agitated by the presence of foreigners in their midst—pastors and missionaries. At this point, our guests were oblivious to the impending danger, but I knew.

"Quick," I told the Banovs, "get the foreigners in the truck, *now*."

Bam! The mob started to throw things at our kids, and to take swings at my pastors. Then they headed toward me to beat me up. This was not a time to be brave. "Now, *now* would be good—get in! Come on everyone, get in the car!"

I am not afraid to die. To live is for Christ, to die is gain (see Phil. 1:21). It is all joy to me, absolutely. It's just that my time was not up. They were coming at me, and this son who messed up for all those years screamed, "Get in the car, Mom! Get in the car!" He became a human shield, and they beat him.

My son received right then the spirit of adoption. It just hit him (literally) square on. He knew who he was, and he knew that it was his joy to risk his life for the Gospel, for his mama. It was the most powerful thing. Eventually we got our group to the police station for protection and to report what had happened. Immediately the police grabbed their AK-47s to search for and destroy the people who beat us, but we pleaded, "Please don't kill them...we forgive them. No, don't kill them!" All through this, my son cried, not because of the pain of his wounds but from the impact of his revelation. "Mom, that was my greatest privilege!"

The police grabbed their AK-47s to search for and destroy the people who beat us.

I keep asking that the God of our Lord Jesus Christ, the glorious Father, may give you the spirit of wisdom and revelation so that you may know Him better, and what is the surpassing greatness of His power toward you. (See Ephesians 1:17-19.)

BELIEVE WHO YOU ARE

An orphan has no inheritance. An adopted child, on the other hand, does. As an adopted child of Father God in Heaven, your inheritance is to command that sickness to die and watch it die. To believe God to multiply food and watch it multiply! To lay your hands on deaf ears, and see them opened; on blind eyes and see them see; on lame legs and see them walk. This is something we see every week of our lives because it is our inheritance! The Book of Acts 29 is not something that we dream about for one day hence. It is *now.* This is here and now. It is our reality because we have stepped away from the orphan mindset. As a result, we can walk forth as daughters and sons laughing at the face of darkness because we know that Christ Jesus lives in us and is greater than the darkness out there. Walk to become the praise of His glory. The power of the Living God belongs to us, and He is worthy, worthy, worthy to be praised. Believe who you are, and everything will transform.

As I stated before, the Lord desires to enlighten the eyes of your heart so that you may know the hope of His calling, the riches of the glory of His inheritance in the saints and His incomparably great power for you. How does that power look, and what is the power for? The power is the working of His mighty strength which He exerted in Christ when He raised Him from the dead.

That the God of our Lord Jesus Christ, the Father of glory, may give to you the spirit of wisdom and revelation in the knowledge of Him, the eyes of your understanding being enlightened; that you may know what is the hope of His calling, what are the riches of the glory of His inheritance in the saints, and what is the exceeding greatness of His power toward us who believe, according to the working of His mighty power which He worked in Christ when He raised Him from the dead and seated Him at His right hand in the heavenly places, far above all principality and power and might and dominion, and every name that is named, not only in this age but also in that which is to come (Ephesians 1:17-21).

God wants to release the riches of His glorious inheritance to you: incredibly great power to love Him, to love Him well, to adore Him, to spend your life in Him...and to crush the serpent's head!

WEDDINGS AND SERPENT ON A STICK

Do you like weddings? We have thousands of them in Mozambique where we have planted over 10,000 churches, glory to God!

The enemy's plan, however, is to stop the weddings, stop the adoptions. In his mind, the plan will work to make orphan spirits of us all, but it won't work when the Body of Christ is woken by the kiss of Jesus. The devil is so stupid!

We were holding a double wedding one Sunday morning for two of our adopted daughters in one of the church plants. Oh how I love weddings! On this particular day, however, as I presented the message, people started to leave. I thought, *What's up with that?* These were my kids, my friends, members of my tribe walking out. They knew me and my ways, so they couldn't have taken offense in any way, at least I hoped not. Families are usually loyal to one another—I love them and they love me, despite my shortcomings! So you can understand my alarm when the trickle became a massive stampede out of the church. Wow, what did I say...did I get the Word wrong?

Suddenly my eldest son, Norberto, who led the worship, leaped off the stage, landed smack in front of me, and bam, whacked the head off a real, live snake. *Well*, I thought, *so much for Point #1!*

Another snake appeared, heading right for me. This time I saw it first, and I whacked its head off. Points 2 and 3 of my message were out the window! So here we had two headless snakes, one of them still wiggling, and two brides lamenting, "A snake, a snake at my wedding!" I tell you, the girls were turning purple! Snakes at your daughters' weddings! Really bad!

"God, what do I do? What do I do? These are our girls, whom we've raised in the Lord, and I really need to know what to do!"

"Stab that snake," He said, "and lift it up on the stick."

Bam! Done. While the snake-with-no-head still wiggled, I screamed, *"We are more than conquerors!"* Amen!

The snakes of this world will not bar the riches of God's inheritance when you step into your full authority as a daughter of the Most High God. You will not live fearful of the snake, unable to step into your inheritance as the daughter bride. Know who you are, and then when you step into that authority, although the snake still wiggles, it is powerless. Beloved of God, it wiggles but is powerless! You need to know that your Father is delighted to back you up. He is not saying, "Oh, I wish she wouldn't get into so much trouble." No, He is backing you up with joy, cheering you on!

The snakes of this world will not bar the riches of God's inheritance when you step into your full authority as a daughter of the Most High God.

Every one of those hundreds of running, screaming, terrified people returned to the wedding when I held up that headless, squirming snake, and we could finally rejoice in the marriage of those two couples!

Our inheritance is incomparably great. His power is powerful enough to raise you from the dead; from the orphan spirit; from the spirit of pain where you feel as though it is never enough; from the spirit of inadequacy that says you are not good enough, not powerful or capable. Pray, "Holy Spirit, come and seal me; seal me, Holy Spirit!"

You Are Alive; You Are Loved

But God, who is rich in mercy, because of His great love with which He loved us, even when we were dead in trespasses, made us alive together with Christ (by grace you have been saved), and raised us up together, and made us sit together in the heavenly places in Christ Jesus, that in the ages to come He might show the exceeding riches of His grace in His kindness toward us in Christ Jesus (Ephesians 2:4-7).

Because of the Father's great love for us, because of His rich mercy, He made us alive, and He is raising you and those whom you love who are dead, today. Listen, in the natural, we have seen literally hundreds and hundreds physically raised, and He can raise *you* out of anything.

It is not difficult for God to raise even an emotionally dead person. If something inside of you has shut down, if you have sinned and feel ashamed, God's great love and rich mercy will cover you. Ask Him, "Lord, forgive me. I want to receive Your mercy." It is as simple as that, a gift that makes you alive. You give Him your heart, and you live. He has made you alive with Christ, even when you were dead in transgressions. By His grace you have been saved, and as such, God raised you up with Christ, seated you with Him in heavenly realms in Christ Jesus so that in the coming ages He might show you the incomparable riches of His grace.

> *It is not difficult for God to raise*
> *even an emotionally dead person.*

About that wayward son of mine who finally shed the orphan spirit although he messed up repeatedly, God said, "Don't divorce him or send him packing. Keep loving him until he understands what grace is."

Yes we disciplined, but we also exuded extraordinary, tenacious, radical love, a love that never died until Norberto finally understood the riches of grace. God expresses that in His kindness toward us.

His grace will take you out of the spirit of an orphan and into the freedom of being a royal daughter, a girl who can dance in the arms of her Father and step on His feet, letting Him walk with her. The joy of being a daughter in her Father's arms never ends!

> *His grace will take you out*
> *of the spirit of an orphan and into*
> *the freedom of being a royal daughter.*

He desires to take you out of a place of dead emotions and a shut-down heart and into the reality of who you are in Him. I ask the Holy Spirit right now as you are reading this to wreck you with an outpouring of His extraordinary grace.

FATHER OF THE BRIDE

God literally goes to the ends of the earth in search of you, then shows you off: "Yes! She's mine! She's mine! I do good work! I chose well. I know who she is, and I chose well!" He does not say, "Oops, I wanted a son, back into the womb you go." You are His blessing. He looks at you through the blood of His Son and says, "She's perfect. Perfect! She's perfect!"

Adoption is not earned either, because it is a gift. God says, "I love you; I want you; I chose you; you are Mine. You are a daughter, you are My beloved, and you are absolutely, ravishingly beautiful to Me."

He has also handpicked you to marry His Son, so trust that He has chosen wisely! If you are a parent, you can relate. You desire the best spouse for your child—one who will unconditionally love, cherish, and adore him or her, forever. Imagine *Father God* choosing *you* to marry *His* Son! That says a lot about who you are and how He thinks about you.

You are a member of His house. You are His workmanship, created in Christ Jesus to do good works which He prepared in advance for you to do (see Eph. 3:10). Now in Christ Jesus, you who were far away have been brought near through the blood of Christ (see Eph. 2:13). Consequently, you are not an orphan or a foreigner or an alien but a fellow citizen with God's people: brothers and sisters in a huge family comprising every tribe, tongue, and nation (see Eph. 2:19).

> *For whom He foreknew, He also predestined to be conformed to the image of His Son, that He might be the firstborn among many brethren. Moreover whom He predestined, these He also called; whom He called, these He also justified; and whom He justified, these He also glorified* (Romans 8:29-30).

I bind every demon of hell in Jesus' name that comes to destroy the spirit of adoption in your life, that attempts to stop the intimate union of Father and child.

Go ahead, beloved, whack off the head of the evil snake—your Daddy God is delighted to back you up!

FREEDOM!

The Lord wants to set you free! If you still feel like an orphan or do not understand who you are in God, I want you to know that the Father wants to hold you today and bless you! He has a key and is unlocking your heart and opening it. Don't be afraid to feel again; don't fear the pain any longer; don't fear stepping on Papa's toes. Let the Lord reach in, deep.

PRAYER

Papa, I need You. I need You to let me know who I am today. I want to be free, a free child: free to dance and free to rejoice, free to take up a sword in my hand, and free to whack the serpent's head off. I want to be free, Papa, to do what You have called me to do, and to step into my destiny. In Jesus' beautiful name. Amen.

Chapter 2

FEEL THE HEARTBEAT OF HEAVEN

by Beni Johnson

One thing I have desired of the Lord, that will I seek:
that I may dwell in the house of the Lord all the days of my life,
to behold the beauty of the Lord,
and to inquire in His temple
(Psalm 27:4).

At the start of the New Year of 1994, Pastor Randy Clark arrived at the tiny Toronto Airport Vineyard Church[1] near Pearson International Airport in Toronto, Canada, for a series of four meetings. By way of a transferable anointing through Randy, the Lord poured out His Spirit upon the church, and it exploded into a lengthy, emotional revival, becoming a hub of renewal. By the autumn of 1995, the revival attracted hundreds of thousands of Christians and Christian leaders from around the world, from almost every nation and denomination.[2]

Within two years, over 9,000 people gave their lives to Christ for the first time. John Arnott, the senior pastor, eventually had to relocate the church to a nearby conference center to accommodate the thousands who poured in every day.[3] Renewal broke out around the world by way of this Toronto Blessing (TB) anointing, transferring through people visiting and spreading the good news upon their arrival home.[4]

You may have heard of the mayhem, as my husband Bill and I did, with reports of worshipers breaking out in laughter and shaking, weeping, groaning, trembling, falling, and staggering under the powerful influence of the Holy Spirit, and in the signs, wonders, miracles, and tangible presence of the Lord felt there. Naturally, Bill went to Toronto to see what was going on. We had been pastoring a small church in the mountains an hour away from our present church, Bethel in Redding, California, when it first started, and what Bill saw in Toronto prompted him to return.

"Let's go," he said, and we headed up north with my parents to the conference. Although we had yet to meet John and Carol Arnott, somehow, we got front seats. At the close of the meeting, I tucked my arm in Bill's, and we headed toward the exit. As we arrived at the rear of the room under the mezzanine, a man who appeared quite drunk in the Spirit,[5] caught my eye and staggered toward us, climbing over people to get to me. He quite literally zapped my arm with a quick touch of his finger, and I flew out of Bill's arms and to the floor as though I had been zinged by a huge bolt of electrical current. For as long as twenty-five minutes, although I was awake and quite aware of what was happening, I could not stop shaking from the "charge." Bill insists he has never seen anything quite like it since.

Just as things started to subside, a woman came up to me and said, "Hi, honey, are you in good shape?"

"Sure," I nodded, "yes."

"More, Lord!" she prayed, and I was "off" again.

Once that Holy Spirit "buzz" wore off enough for me to walk, Bill and my dad each grabbed an arm and helped me with the quarter mile walk back to our hotel, where I "sobered up" just fine, thank you!

The following day we attended the conference again, but it was strange because, while Bill loves the front, we sat in the back row near that mezzanine!

"What happened to me last night, God?" I inquired.

Whoosh, down I went *again,* but this time in a heap of tears.

"Last evening," said the Lord, "I was pulling lies out of you, shaking out those things that you thought were lies, birthing anew in you who you really are!"

It transformed me.

A similar thing had happened before at a women's conference we were hosting back home, where I was scheduled to speak. I had been nervously sitting in the back of the venue awaiting my turn at the podium, scared out of my mind. Imagine, the pastor's wife struck with stage fright!

Although I knew somehow that
what was happening was good,
I did not have a clue what it was.

The Holy Spirit suddenly came upon me in much the same way and down I went, weeping. The weeping turned into deep, heart-wrenching cries, then serious travail. Although I knew somehow that what was happening was good, I did not have a clue what it was. I did know something was up and sensed the Lord transforming something.

DIVINE LOVE METAMORPHOSIS

I grew up with a very quiet spirit, labeled "shy" by many as a result. My parents knew this was not true, but others thought so simply because I wasn't chatty. Shyness eventually did become such a stronghold in my life that I developed difficulty communicating. You could not pay me enough to get up in front of a crowd and speak. In school, if I had an oral exam, I preferred to get a failing grade than to take it. Thus, you see, the Lord delivered me of that stronghold, and I have not stopped talking since!

This is not to say that satan did not try to assail me again. He didn't say, "Oh, hands off now; I can't touch Beni anymore. I can't feed her that lie." Many times he tried to feed me the garbage, but because the Lord had delivered me from the stronghold of extreme shyness, I was now equipped with the tool to say, "No, that is *not* who I am!

If, after deliverance, the enemy comes at you with a familiar spirit (which can be quite subtle because he does not play fair), you are equipped to say, "That is not me anymore! I don't have to live there."

Following that Toronto weeping episode, someone just had to *mention* the name of Jesus, or share a testimony of renewal, and I'd weep and weep. This entire process, I am convinced, was one of a gradual falling in love with the Holy Spirit, and the beginning of intercessory ministry.

As a youngster raised in the church, I had always loved Jesus and God the Father, but I had never ever experienced this intense infatuation with the love of the Holy Spirit.

During this process of love transformation, Bill and I were asked to pastor Bethel Church, which was the church I had attended as a little girl, from two years old on! In those days, we had to be voted in by the board or congregation, and we underwent a number of interviews, and some waiting. I was confident we would pastor that church, but it took Bill quite a while longer to have that assurance. It was a difficult time because I was in a spiritually emotional state already, and not being able to tell anyone in our church about our move just escalated it all. I am sure everyone thought I was a mess! We got the appointment, but I wasn't surprised; it just had to happen!

At first Bill commuted to Redding, so once he left in the morning, and I got the kids got off to high school, I'd rest in the Lord at home, play worship music, and just get lost in God. No agenda; I just wanted Him! In short, I grew addicted to His love, finding myself in the secret place of His presence, craving more of His precious Spirit with each passing day. This kind of addiction is good for you! Once you get a taste of His love, you are never the same. Once you hear Him say, "I love you," you are wrecked!

LOVE TOUCHDOWN

The move from a 260 member church to a congregation of 2,200 was a little scary, and I was like, "Help us, Jesus!" I told my mom (my parents were the church elders), "I can't be like the last pastor's wife, OK? I'm not her; that's not me."

"Honey," Mom encouraged, "just be yourself."

That was the best advice she ever gave me. I have been myself ever since!

Unfortunately, we lost about a thousand people in the changeover and renewal. One night Bill gave an altar call and invited the remaining congregation up, those who had been in "hiding," weary as they were without a pastor overseeing things for nine months, and then through the changeover. Of the hardy 150 or so who came forward, one in particular caught my eye, an old friend whom I had not seen for years. The Lord hit her as He hit me in Toronto. *Zap*, down she went. Bill and I looked at each other, grinned, and said, "We've got it! Here we go!"

*We didn't expect such a move
to happen so quickly,
but God was in a hurry.*

We didn't expect such a move to happen so quickly, but God was in a hurry. We leaned into the Holy Spirit and watched Him take that huge ship and turn its course. Everything that needed to die in that place from that day on, died, and the Lord resurrected things anew with His refreshing Spirit.

BIRTH OF INTERCESSION

The Lord began, in our times of intimacy, to show me things in the spirit realm to be praying about. I would see people, cities, happenings, and situations, and in agreement with Him, say, "That's a great idea, God. Let's go there and do that." Or, "It would be great for You to heal that person."

One day, I "saw" a picture in my mind of someone I had never seen before. I just prayed in the spirit concerning him and knew that God was answering. Increasingly, my prayers were being answered, and I realized that I had, indeed, become an intercessor.

That transformation by the Holy Spirit changed the whole course of my life! Until that time, I was never really involved in ministry beyond raising my children as a stay-at-home mom, which was a dream in itself! It was wonderful to be raising world changers, tucking our children in at night with the promise that they could do anything through God's power. Becoming an intercessor was a bonus, and it was birthed from that intimate place I had developed with the Lord.

People ask me all the time, "How do you do it all—handle all that being a mom, wife, and leader entails?" And I just say, "Time with God. More than just reading the Bible and uttering a quick prayer, but storing up a well, a perpetual reserve of intimacy, to draw on. It comes by way of knowing God and His presence."

THE HEAVENLY REALM

When I arrived at Bethel, people started coming to me with dreams and visions of the first-and-second-realms nature. (The *first* realm is what we can see with the physical eye; it is what we see here on earth in the natural. The *second* is the angelic and demonic realm, and the *third* is the glory realm, which is the holy realm, the throne room of God.)

They were dreaming earthquakes, demons, war, you name it, and I thought, *This can't be right; what do we do with all this stuff?* God then gave me a word at a conference in Albany, Oregon, through the prophet Bob Jones, who had called all prophetic intercessors into a private meeting. He told us to stop prophesying or interceding out of the first two realms, and instead, get ourselves into the third realm of Heaven, and prophesy from the throne room vantage point looking down upon the other two realms. In that third, Holy-of-holies realm of Heaven, you are seated with Christ, co-partnering with God. If there is a situation or something that needs to be dealt with, you are right there asking the Lord about it, and receiving throne room strategy.

Although Bill cannot stand to watch the news for very long, I do, and note many of the world's concerns in my prayer journal. Then, I access the throne room for strategy concerning how to pray. "What's up with that, Lord?" I'll ask, and He will give me insight and direction.

> *What we see in the natural realm*
> *is often just the surface*
> *of what is going on in the deeper sense.*

What we see in the natural realm is often just the surface of what is going on in the deeper sense, so we really don't always know how to effectively pray or prophesy. Often the Father shows me the root cause of a situation or problem.

THRONE ROOM STRATEGY

Many years ago, the Lord gave Bill a vision for a twenty-four-hour prayer house. "We have to build this house," he said to the board. Imagine his surprise when one of the board members said, "I'll show you the plans; I drew them up two years ago!"

Both he and Bill had received the same vision, so it was apparent the project had to get the go-ahead. Everything went smoothly in the building and in its financing. We don't use it for anything other than what God showed us: not corporate prayer, weddings, deliverances. It is a soaking place with God.

One day, I received word from some of our people that the prayer room was under demonic spiritual attack, and we actually hired additional security. "Lord," I prayed, "I need direction on this; I don't know what to do, but I do know it has to stop. Please help me figure it out."

The following morning I was reading the weather page of the newspaper and noticed for the first time, in a small corner of the report, information concerning the dates and times of the phases of the moon: new, first quarter, full, and last or third quarter. Later, when I went back to where I had left off in my Bible devotions, I read:

> *Sing aloud to God our strength; make a joyful shout to the God of Jacob. Raise a song and strike the timbrel, the pleasant harp with the lute. Blow the trumpet at the time of the New Moon, at the full moon, on our solemn feast day* (Psalm 81:1-3).

Wow, I took that as strategy straight from Heaven. "OK, Lord, I take this to mean we are to wait for the first new moon, and blow the shofar at sunrise."

I only revealed this to Bill and to a friend whom I asked to accompany me to the prayer house on that new moon morning. At sunrise we blew the shofar and left. A week later, I talked to the security people and asked how things were going.

"Funny you should ask," he said. "All the weird stuff stopped."

WISDOM AND REVELATION

We had an employee whose son had been a drug runner. One day she asked if I would talk to him. "He really wants to talk to you and has some things to tell you concerning what's happening in the area."

When he and I finally met, this unsaved youth surprised me with information about all the drug dealings going on in our regions: the Mexican cartels, the grow ops in the mountains, the whole business.

"OK, Lord," I said after he had left. "I have all this information. Why, I don't know. Now what? How do we pray strategically over this first realm stuff? How do we take care of this problem?"

The next morning I awoke convinced that I knew what to do. *Take the shofar to the border.* At the start of the next moon phase, I took a friend with me for the drive to the Oregon/California state line. We arrived there early in the morning and blew the shofar in the direction of the California Valley. Back in the car we prayed, and the following prayer flowed out of me: God, forgive us for allowing a *sorcery spirit* access to our region.

Sorcery? At first I could not see a connection. Later, I discovered that sorcery in the New Testament Greek is connected to drugs (see Gal. 5:20). The word used for sorcery is *pharmakeia,* from which we derive our word *pharmacy.* Those experimenting with illegal drugs today probably do not realize that they are also experimenting with witchcraft. As such, if you are praying for an addicted user, a possible strategic key would be to break off the spirit of witchcraft.

> *Those experimenting with illegal drugs today probably do not realize that they are also experimenting with witchcraft.*

One week later the paper reported multiple drug dealer and cartel busts, confiscations, and drug arrests in our region. It is incredible how a simple prayer for direction can lead to such transformation. And by the way, this young man is now saved, glory to God.

EFFECTIVE PRAYER

Who said prayer has to be boring? Downloads from God in Heaven are remarkable if you Feel the Heartbeat of Heaven and know what it is to be ruined by how much God loves all people on this earth, good and bad. The Father's heart is for humankind. His heart, if you have ever been in the intimate place and felt it beat for the lost, ruins you for life. Your answer to the impossible is in that incredible realm of the secret place of His love presence where God has an answer for everything.

As an intercessor, I often interchange between hope prayers, faith prayers, and love prayers. *Hope prayers*, where we petition God (begging is more like it!), are good, but I want to suggest to you that you move also from hope to faith, from hoping something will happen to knowing it will happen. We see hope prayers in the story of the persistent widow who begged and begged the unjust judge until he finally said in exasperation, "OK, OK, you can have it!" (see Luke 18:1-8).

Faith prayers are prayers of declaration. When Jesus was in the boat sleeping through a storm, the terrified disciples awakened Him: "Help, Lord!" Christ turned to the storm and commanded it to be still.

"Where is your faith?" He asked. Indeed, Jesus answered their prayers of help because they asked Him to, but I am convinced that His true intent was to have them command the winds to stop. (See Mark 4:35-41; Luke 8:22-25.)

When I am in my prayer closet and in the intimate place with the Lord, I petition Him, but I also move into faith because faith moves mountains. Yes, petition up a storm, but also stand in that place of faith and make declarations.

You get to that place of faith and belief through *love prayers*, which emerge from the deepest and most intimate place of intimate worship, out of that deep inner place of adoration from within your spirit. This is how you get the *uumphhf* in you that will declare what the Lord is doing so that you can prophesy into something and know that it will happen. You have been in the realm of the secret place of His presence, where you know the Father's intentions. It is that place where you step into faith that believes that it will happen and that it will be.

THE LOVE PLACE

The secret place is where we soak in His presence and hang out with God. As desperate as you may be for His tangible presence, striving is not rest, so just rest in Him. Relax, breathe in His Holy Spirit, and let everything out. Worship music may help you focus away from what to make for Sunday dinner and onto Him. We don't soak to bring forth an agenda, or enter into it asking for anything other than God Himself.

The secret place is where we soak in His presence and hang out with God.

I recall reading a story about a heart surgeon training his interns while doing an actual heart surgery. Beside him, hooked up to machines, was the patient's old heart and the new donor heart. Before he transplanted the new heart, the doctor placed both together to sync the heartbeats. They connected, the two hearts beat as one, and he finished the operation.

This is what happens in the soaking place of God's presence. Your hearts begin to beat as one! Usually after such a time of our hearts beating in unison, I move into intercession because now I am praying from the very heart of the Father.

You just never know what will happen when you encounter God in your devoted time together. One youth leader reported the Lord taking him back to the beginning of creation to watch as the Creator spoke everything into existence. Now that would be amazing. You may just fall asleep, and God will minister to your spirit while you are "out," or He may give you dreams or visions. One thing for sure, He will give your heart tremendous peace. The *shalom* of Heaven passes all understanding. In transition, especially, it is a beautiful thing!

God is always up to something, so it's best to put control into His hands. Declare that He is in full control and that you will no longer be afraid, in the name of Jesus. Then, put your hands on your heart and say, "Yes" to all that He is doing in your life.

PRAYER

Father, please give us a heart transplant; change the rhythm, the way the blood pumps into our veins. Sync our hearts with Your own. In Jesus' name.

ENDNOTES

1. Now known as Toronto Airport Christian Fellowship. Located at 272 Attwell Drive, Toronto, Ontario, Canada,

M9W 6M3. Please visit their Web site at www.tacf.org. They are still in revival!

2. This information is adapted from an article on the TACF (Toronto Airport Christian Fellowship) Web site (www. tacf.org/about/revival/history) regarding the Toronto Blessing. The copyright information from that Web site is as follows:

Acknowledgment: This information is adapted from an article by Daina Doucet which appeared in Spread the Fire, January/February 1995, Volume 1, Issue 1. Copyright 1995 by the Toronto Airport Vineyard. Revised version Copyright 1996 by the Toronto Airport Christian Fellowship. All rights reserved. Information accessed January 16, 2010.

3. Ibid.

4. Ibid.

5. Regarding the phenomena of being drunk in the spirit, please see Acts 2:5-13, where the crowd who had gathered from many different nations marveled because they heard the disciples speaking in their own languages. Some accused the disciples of being drunk on wine, but Peter admonished them, quoting the prophet Joel in verse 17: *"'And it shall be in the last days,' God says, 'That I will pour forth of My Spirit on all mankind...'"* (NASB). See also Ephesians 5:18: *"Do not get drunk on wine, for that is dissipation, but be filled with the Spirit"* (NASB).

Chapter 3

HOT BATHS AND CHEESE, AND FRESH BREAD PLEASE

by *Heidi Baker*

Lavish: To bestow something in generous or
extravagant quantities upon; to cover something thickly
or liberally. Give freely to, spend generously on, heap on,
shower with; liberal, bountiful, openhanded,
unsparing, extravagant.
Origin: late Middle English
(as a noun denoting profusion); from
Old French *lavasse* meaning deluge of rain,
from *laver* meaning to wash.[1]

"Can everyone please clear the building right away?" boomed a voice over the conference room loudspeaker. The meeting[2] had run overtime, and the cleaning crew and venue staff wanted to close up so they could get home.

I wanted to leave, really I did. I am a rascal, but an obedient one, and desired to accommodate their request. However, I couldn't move my legs, arms, or even turn my head. When Randy Clark prayed for me earlier, I went down, and there I lay for the rest of the evening, stuck to the floor by the power of God in a corner of the room.

The security guard hit the microphone again, pleading. "Listen, I really mean it. I need everyone here to get up *now*. Have mercy on us. We all work hard. It is very late!"

What was I to do? I felt paralyzed and heavy, and even worse, I couldn't talk! *God, please help me!* I did not want to further frustrate the security guard. If she saw me still there on the floor not having moved even a muscle—oh!

God answered. "Heidi, I am sending a very precious servant, someone who is very close to My heart, someone who touches Me very deeply. I am sending her to rescue you!"

> *I did not want to further frustrate the security guard.*
> *If she saw me still there on the floor*
> *not having moved even a muscle—oh!*

I wondered who it might be. Most people had gone home. *It couldn't be the guard. God said it would be a servant...oh my, I felt tender and vulnerable...I didn't want her mad at me—oh no—she's headed this way!*

"Hi, Sweetie," she said, surprising me by her understanding tone. "We've seen this before. Don't worry; it's OK. I'll get some people to help."

"Betty" found four people from the church to haul me into a van, carry me to my hotel room, and plop me on the bed.[3] The next morning four people arrived, picked me up, hauled me into the van, carried me to the venue, and (gently) plopped me back on the floor. For several days these amazing, tender servants of God took care of me because I was totally helpless and dependent upon them for all of my needs, and ones that I could not even express. Miraculously, whenever I thought of something, like needing water, or having to go to the restroom, people showed up to help, and eventually even brought me a wheelchair.

God's point in all this?

"You can do nothing without Me."

I thought, "But God, I know that! I've already worked in the mission fields for eons, preached the Gospel since I was sixteen!"

He replied, "You can do nothing without the Body of Christ, as well."

That, I did *not* know, nor did I want to hear it, but I wasn't exactly positioned to wrestle with God. Still, my thoughts raced. *I don't always like the Body of Christ; they're not always nice, don't always have a heart for the poor, the dying, the wretched, the lame, the orphan, the widow; they can be selfish, frivolous, and they eat a lot, and I don't know if...I wish...oh!*

LITTLE MISSIONARY IN THE DIRT

As a "severe" missionary (and Rolland a third-generation missionary), we were good at suffering, good at making things hard. As a result, I just did not understand the Church in the West. We lived in slums—with the dying. Missionaries in Asia especially seemed to compete to see who suffered the most. To be miserable was almost a prerequisite to becoming a missionary. We strictly adhered to a poverty mindset, and rer than the poor, skinnier than the poor, and always hungry, all the while loving Jesus with all of our heart, enough to die for Him. We got the dying part just right!

We lived in slums—with the dying.

I remember how upset I was with the "frivolous" Body of Christ and how often I'd think, *Oh please, what are you doing? Can you see the poor? Is something wrong with you?* We were so dedicated to misery that we would not allow ourselves to have hot water because only the rich had hot water. We worked with the poor, so we poured cold water over our kids' heads out of a bucket from the ninth floor of a slum building. They needed inner healing for that! We should have gotten hot water. It would have been cheaper, but no, we were going to be the most miserable missionaries on the planet and smile about it because we die for God! And we didn't eat cheese because cheese was for the "frivolous" who spent their money on nonsense, and I loved cheese. Even today, I would rather eat cheese than anything else.

Don't get me wrong. I am content serving the Lord and sleeping in "billion star" hotels, in the open, in the dirt, no cheese, no water, hot or cold. If I have a bottle of water, I take a sip and share the rest of it with a hundred people. My problem was that I just could not shed that impoverished, orphan mindset so that I could also enjoy Papa-to-daughter bounty.

I am content serving the Lord and sleeping
in "billion star" hotels, in the open,
in the dirt, no cheese, no water, hot or cold.

I know, many of you who have heard me speak are used to seeing me sliding down the wall, but I want you to understand how God apprehended this little missionary. He knocked me to the floor after seventeen years of living and ministering with this orphan mindset. He said, "Now you are really dead, Heidi! Soon you'll get up and do something for joy's sake!"

I didn't know that God was really my Father, that He so understood me that He knew how I loved soaking in hot baths and eating cheese. He just knew that, and He knew that I was tired. He knew that I just needed to soak, and He knew what would touch my little girl's heart inside. Oh, yes, He is thrilled for the over one million people whom we have led to Jesus. Oh yes, He is thrilled about it, but He also cares about me. It is so much better now than it used to be!

EPIPHANY!

I have trouble learning things quickly. The Lord was allowing me to learn the lesson in a way that I would never forget. He wanted Saul's armor *off*. I was the missionary who won the misery prize, and He really wanted to apprehend her.

I recall being carried into the elevator on a luggage cart; people who were on the elevator didn't know me, and, thinking I was deaf as well as quadriplegic, were saying, "They should get that poor woman a chair! Oh, how sad that she's paralyzed like that; look at her, poor soul can't move."

I was thinking, *God, **what** is going on here...could You....*

Very clearly, the Lord responded. "Ephesians."

What was I to do? I couldn't get a Bible, much less lift one to read. I longed to get someone to read the Book of Ephesians to me, to see what the Lord was saying, but I couldn't speak.

> *What was I to do?*
> *I couldn't get a Bible,*
> *much less lift one to read.*

The floor itself was uncomfortably and painfully hard, and I thought how great it would be just to have a pillow. Then, just like that, four people showed up to carry me to a comfortable room. After they propped me on the couch with cushions, they brought my husband Rolland to me. He had been so worried because, of course, I could not eat either.

But all I was interested in at the point was to communicate to him that I wanted him to read me the Bible. With all my strength, I was just able to whisper the first word I'd spoken in days, "Ephesians!"

THE LAVISHER

My eyes poured with tears as Rolland read from Ephesians 1:4-14, and the words breathed life into me. God Himself chose us; He *chose* us in Him before the creation of the world to be holy and blameless in His sight. He chose us to be holy and pure. He picked us in love. How? In love! He *predestined* us to be *adopted* as sons and daughters through Jesus Christ in accordance with His pleasure and His will to the praise of His glorious grace, which He has freely given us in the One He loves. In Him, we have redemption through the blood, the forgiveness of sins in accordance with the riches of God's grace that He *lavished on us!* (See Ephesians 1:4-14.)

Lavish is never a tiny thing...

Lavish is never a little bit...

HE PICKED YOU TO LAVISH ON

Lavish is extraordinarily, abundantly, amazingly overflowing. God wants to lavish on you! He wants you, He picked you, He chose you, and He loves you lavishly. What did He lavish on you? The riches of God's grace. With all wisdom and understanding, He made known to us the mystery of His will according to His good pleasure which He purposed in Christ to be put into affect when the times will have reached their fulfillment to bring all things in Heaven and on earth together under one head, even Christ. God has lavished grace on us. These words were like a hot, fiery branding iron burning into my heart. Every word Rolland read over and over, and each one burned and burned and burned into my heart, searing deeply into my soul. I thought, *I'm adopted! God loves me!* My thoughts then turned to our children, to all the Mozambican children we've adopted into our home, and God said, "I want you to believe Me, to take every child that I put in front of you."

"Yes, Lord."

"I want you to see this as a prophetic sign that I have literally gone and searched the earth, and I have chosen every man, woman, and child. All they need to do is say 'yes' back to Me."

This shook me up because I've seen this on the mission field. We go out and call the orphan, the broken, the dying, and we say, "Come home." Do you realize that some of them don't want to? Some come home and go back and get dirty again. They jump back into the garbage, back into the dirt, back into filth. But those who say, "Yes" are transformed by the glory of God's love, by lavish, radical grace! God wants you to say "Yes" to His lavish love.

Lavish love.

Lavish love.

Lavish love.

One day at home I was excitedly preparing a party for those very ones the Lord placed in front of me: the poor, crippled, blind, broken-hearted. So many came that there wasn't enough food to go around. I recall looking at the salad I had prepared, which was a major luxury, and crying out to God, "What are we going to do? We don't have enough, and we can't buy more."

The coolest thing happened.

> *Salad poured over the edges of the pan—constantly increasing, volumes of it.*

"Look, look at the salad," people started screaming. "Look at it, *look at it!*" Salad poured over the edges of the pan—constantly increasing, volumes of it, and the bowl overflowed with lettuce and vegetables. We had more when we finished than when we started.

"Just take the leftovers home, take them home, take them home!" That's lavish, the grace of God!

FREEDOM FOR LITTLE ORPHAN HEIDI

Well, you would think I'd have learned my lesson, but that orphan spirit tried to sneak up and grab me again. The word of the Lord for me was, "The nations," and I was thinking, *No!*

But my children, fifty of them with me at the time, screamed *"Yes! Get her, God. Pour it on!"* God and the kids won.

As a result of this divine mandate, I had another conference in the West and was booked into a posh hotel by the organizers. The contrast from bush to luxury was too much for me. I had fire ant bites all over my body, had traveled for three days, had even scrubbed my toenails to get there, and this fellow shows me my room, complete with Jacuzzi. A hot tub in the living room, of all things! I lost it. "Frivolous, frivolous!" I said. "You could just put me in a Motel 6." I'm thinking, *Feed the poor, feed the poor, don't they know to feed the poor? A Jacuzzi!*

> *The contrast from bush to luxury was too much for me.*

"Couldn't you just put me in...a simple room?"

The guy swung his head around, totally exasperated, and let me have it. "Don't you know that we are trying to bless you? Can't you just *receive* the *blessing?* Do you know you make us feel bad? Take a hot bath."

"Sorry," I said, while turning on the bath water. Well, I couldn't get enough of it; I think I had five soaks that day and every day, wasting water, bubbling it up between every session, and *thoroughly* enjoying it.

God understands us, and He wants to break that orphan spirit from us forever. That doesn't mean to soak twenty times a day at the expense of what God has called you to do. I have been tromping in the bush now for fifteen years, and it is my joy to sleep in the dirt, to walk for hours in the sun, to hold babies with scabies and lice, rock them in my arms, and go into the darkest places on the planet and see God move. It is my joy. I count it all joy because once I truly understood what it was to be a daughter, I was *free* to *lay it all down*, free just to give it all away or receive anything God wanted for me. There was always enough love around then because I finally died as an orphan and arose as an adopted daughter of the Father. His grace *poured* through me. I was free to eat the cheese, soak in the tub, or lie in the dirt with the fire ants. I pray that the eyes of your heart also would be enlightened.

No more miserable missionaries. No more miserable ministers. No more miserable daughters! Only laid-down lovers of the Father, lovers of the Son, possessed by the Holy Spirit. It is our joy to run into the darkness and watch it disappear. Let His grace pour through you. Arise, beautiful daughter, arise!

Prayer

Father, we want to be transformed; we are hungry again, thirsty again. God, oh God, we want fresh bread, the fresh bread, Jesus! Give us fresh bread, Papa! Give us wine from Heaven to drink. Don't leave us like this. We want to be different now than we were a moment ago. Lord, not a single stale crumb to my readers. I pray for the fragrance of fresh bread to fill the atmosphere, for You to fill our homes with Your presence, with Your glory, with Your kingdom, with Your angelic beings.

We cry out, "More Lord, more Lord, more bread and cheese, please!" We are Your adopted and sealed children! We join the chorus of Heaven, gladly praising you. Hosanna! Hallelujah! Possess us Father, in Jesus' name.

Endnotes

1. *New Oxford American Dictionary,* ed. Erin McKean (New York: Oxford UP, USA, 2005); *Oxford American Writer's Thesaurus,* comp. by Christine Lindberg (New York: Oxford UP, USA, 2008), s.v. "Lavish."

2. With Randy Clark in Toronto, Ontario, Canada, in about 1995.

3. Betty is still a friend today after fifteen years!

Chapter 4

LOVE AMBUSH: CONNECTING THE DOTS OF HIS PASSION!

by Winnie "CoCo" Banova

When the Lord puts passion in your heart for something, eventually you figure out the desires that you have are His. Because He is in you, He releases their burn, and they begin to blend with your own thoughts and ideas. Sometimes it takes awhile for the big picture to emerge, but it is during that inevitable moment, when all the dots connect, that you realize God has set you up. The Lord has prepared you and plowed the way for you. He has put people and resources in your life to help you, and now everything begins to make sense.

In Luke 24, we find two men on the road to Emmaus just days after Jesus had been crucified and buried. As they were walking, the resurrected Jesus showed up and said, "What is going on, guys? You look really sad."

They were so disillusioned and confused. "Haven't you heard? You must be a stranger!" they replied.

Jesus kept His poker face and said, "Tell Me what happened; fill Me in."

"We thought that Jesus was going to get us all out of the mess we were in." When they were finished telling their sad story, He began speaking and opened up the Word to them. They liked what they were hearing and asked Him to stay awhile longer. He agreed, and they sat down to eat together. All of a sudden, their scaly eyes were opened. Jesus revealed Himself and they now saw that it was the Resurrected One who was speaking with them all along. What a marvelous reunion! Then in the blink of an eye, Jesus disappeared.

> *We thought that Jesus was going to get us all out of the mess we were in.*

This "vanishing act" bothered me for quite some time. I asked, "Lord, why didn't You stay with them for a while and hang out? You labored with them all of that time. You were there, and they finally 'got it,' but then You disappeared. You didn't even hang out for dessert."

Finally He helped me connect the dots. They were kept from recognizing Jesus *on purpose*—Jesus was teaching them a new form of communication. On their way back to Jerusalem, they were talking to each other and saying, *"Were not our hearts burning within us? Were not our hearts burning when He was speaking to us?"* He was teaching them to recognize the burning of the Word in their hearts, and His burning passion in their spirits. Since Jesus was no longer going to walk around with them in His earthly body, they had to start learning this new communication system right away.

It's a Set-Up—Desire and Destiny Go Hand in Hand

Pay attention to those burning passions and desires, for you have no idea the places that they will take you to. As you follow their lead, you will find yourself doing exactly what God has called you to do.

A few years ago, the Lord said to me, "I need you to pay attention. The desire for you to go to the garbage dump is something that I have placed within you. It's My desire. *My* desire." *Now* I have connected the dots: "Yes, I will go!" But let me back up and tell you the story.

When I look back, the first pulse of desire took place thirty-five years ago before I married my husband. A girlfriend and I were co-leading a missionary team in Mexico. We shared a burning compassion for the poor, and during our day off, we decided to investigate the poor who were living at the garbage dump in Tijuana, just the two of us.

> *Neither of us could speak Spanish to ask for directions, but eventually it made sense to follow a garbage truck.*

Neither of us could speak Spanish to ask for directions, but eventually it made sense to follow a garbage truck. Before we knew it, we found ourselves sandwiched in our little car between huge, intimidating, dump trucks caravanning up to the top of the mountain of garbage. I tell you, we were in for a surprise; we had no clue. We couldn't have turned around if we wanted to, and we certainly were not prepared for what we saw—an entire community of people living in the most awful, unimaginable conditions. At that very moment, I was baptized into garbage dump ministry.

DRAWN BY FLAMING COMPASSION: TIME TO CONNECT THE BIG DOTS

It wasn't until many years later that I returned to a garbage dump. We were on one of our first visits to Mozambique, getting ready to do missionary work with Heidi and Rolland Baker.

We had purchased a bottle of perfume as a special gift for Heidi who said, "Oh, thank you, I am going to wear this someplace *very* special."

Where do you think she wore it? Early the next morning she walked out of her room in a beautiful blue dress and a cloud of scent and said, "Let's go to the Maputo garbage dump; let's go!" Her team was made up of about five or six of her children, plus George and me and our daughter Yana. What a ragamuffin team! But we went, and it was remarkable. I felt something so familiar for me there. And as I watched the liquid love pour out of Heidi as she ministered to the people there, I literally felt my heart burn within me. I remembered my trip to the dump of Tijuana so many years before, and I realized that I was being drawn by a flaming passion that came from God's very own heart.

Up to this point, our passion for the poor had already been building. Our ministry, Global Celebration, had been ministering to the poor, rejected Gypsies of Bulgaria communities for years and years. Through another series of dot connections, we found ourselves committed to the orphans and destitute of Nicaragua as well. Now there we were in another part of the world: Mozambique and Malawi. My passion for the poor was already aflame. Seeing Heidi in action was like pouring kerosene on my fire, and the passion inside my heart became a blazing inferno. It was inevitable that this desire was steering me back to the garbage dumps of the world. This had been another big dot that I needed to see, to feel, to experience—this outpouring of irresistible love. To this day, I am grateful to God for Heidi and Rolland's display of fearless, compelling love that helped me to connect the most magnificent of dots.

Since then, the Lord has increased our ministry's focus toward the poorest of the poor and expanded our reach throughout more of the third world. Now we find ourselves traveling across so many time zones, bringing the love of Christ wherever we can. Sometimes we do planned, organized evangelistic outreaches where we bring the people their favorite food and music, and sometimes we do surprise visits and "love ambush" them as we show up in the middle of an ordinary day. There are so many stories to tell, but I will choose just a few to show you how simple connecting the dots can be if you are really paying attention.

While on a layover in Frankfurt, Germany, I picked up a *Vogue* magazine sitting on the table next to me in the airport lounge. Immediately I was drawn to an article about the Gypsies in Romania. I read about a mother who was extremely proud of her two boys now that they were foraging through the city dump for things that they could recycle, things they could fix and sell to make a living. For her family, this was a big step up in life because previously they had lived as street thieves. As I was reading their story, my heart burst into an urgent, flaming fire, and I said, "I have to go—I have to find these treasures!"

We had already been ministering to the rejected Gypsies of Bulgaria for years, and I knew that Romania was right over the border. "George," I said to my husband, "I *have* to find those Gypsies. Next time we go to Bulgaria, let's pop into Bucharest."

Week after week, my heart increasingly burned for the Gypsies I had read about. I grew restless and could not sleep thinking about them. It became obvious that I wouldn't be able to wait the six- or seven-month time span before our next trip back there—I had to go *now!*

Now that this fiery dot was connected, I immediately started to get some money together and make my plans. A few friends heard about what I was doing and joined me, taking their vacation time and paying their own way.

"The Signs" and How to Read Them

We flew to Bulgaria, picked up two of our Bulgarian and Gypsy pastor friends, and drove across the Romanian border in search of our Gypsies. We had difficulty finding them as we drove our van down countless streets. It was almost the end of the day when suddenly, at the end of one road, we saw a Romanian man frantically signaling and warning us with his hands *not* to go a certain way. He was probably thinking that we were lost tourists innocently headed into a dangerous place.

"That's it, that's the sign; that is our road sign..." I eagerly blurted out. "Thanks for the directions!"

We screeched to a glorious stop as though we had just found the mother of all sales at Nordstrom. Sure enough, the road that he told us not to go down was the very road that led us straight into the Gypsy camp. After parking, we walked into the camp and found four men hanging out near the entrance.

*We screeched to a glorious stop as though
we had just found the mother of all sales at Nordstrom.*

"Hi," I said, boldly walking right up to one of them and reaching out to shake his hand. I wanted them to know that our visit was intentional, but the scruffy fellow and his friends gave us a look that said, *Don't touch us—can't you see we are dirty?* At that point, some offered their cleaner elbows to shake.

Venturing further into their little community, it appeared that we were standing in the middle of a junkyard. Car parts, old sewing machines, and all sorts of assorted scraps and recyclables were strewn all over the ground in separated piles. Ramshackle corrugated tin homes were everywhere, and a few children peeked at us through their burlap doorways.

We walked toward a small gathering of Gypsy women and again introduced ourselves. "We are not lost, oh no," our mannerisms said as we reached out to them in love, for we could not speak the language.

They cried out, "We know that you have a message for us!"

Their jubilant reaction surprised us; we could not believe how thrilled they seemed to see us and almost at first wondered if our two translators (a Bulgarian Gypsy pastor and a Bulgarian pastor) had relayed things correctly back to us. Right away, I shared with them through the translators how we had driven from Bulgaria and around the city all day long looking for them, how we had come from America, how we had read about them three months before, and how we had declared our intent and resolve to find them. This thrilled them more. What a spectacle it was! One of the women even brought out a Romanian Bible, which we later learned she had found only a short time before our arrival while picking through the garbage.

You can know Him and His presence.
You can have a baptism of fire!

In this whirlwind of excitement, we gathered the women and children, and I preached the simple Gospel message to them. "God gave His Son for you, to wash you inside and cleanse you from your sin so that His Spirit could live inside of you." Encouragingly, I added. "You can know Him and His presence. You can have a baptism of fire!"

We laid hands on them and prayed and hugged them too. They wept, they cried, they laughed, they sang. We wept, we cried, we laughed, we sang with them—the entire gathering feeling the presence of the Holy Spirit and His love.

Two months later, we discovered why they were so excited. Remember that Bible the woman found? Every day she and the others would gather in the common grassy area where they did their laundry to read it. Finding it hard to decipher, they had been crying out to God: "Please, find us someone; send us someone!"

You know the rest of the story. God said, "Yes, I have just the girl. I will work up this deal for you; just you wait!" That was in 2005, and we've been going back there ever since.

What a dot connection! Isn't that amazing? Religion may tell you to be afraid of your heart, but I say pay attention to those burning desires in your heart because the Lord Himself has placed them there. They are His desires whetting your desires in the deepest places of your heart.

Once His desire gets inside of you,
something happens, and your heart is set aflame.

Once His desire gets inside of you, something happens, and your heart is set aflame. You are irresistibly drawn to these places, and you cannot stay away. Thirty-five years after my visit to Tijuana, I am actively pursuing the people who live off of the garbage dumps of the world.

THE GARBAGE DUMP PSALM

God wants to be acknowledged. He wants to receive the glory due His name.

Imagine my surprise when I found a Scripture referring to the needy living in the *garbage dump*, that exact terminology, in the Passover Song of Psalm 113, New Living Translation Bible. The King James Version terms it *ash heap*, and other translations render it as *garbage pile* or *heap of rubbish*. I encourage you as I do, to seek out the fullness of the Word through the reading of many official Bible translations to increase your revelation and understanding of it. Something new may just open up to you.

(Imagine Jesus singing the words as you read these verses):

> *Who can be compared with the Lord our God, who is enthroned on high? He stoops to look down on heaven and on earth. He lifts the poor from the dust and the needy from the garbage dump. He sets them among princes, even the princes of His own people! He gives the childless woman a family, making her a happy mother. Praise the Lord!* (Psalm 113:5-9 NLT)

Wow! Of course I called Heidi. "Heidi, Heidi! This is for you! This is the legal word! It's legal! The Word really terms it 'garbage dump'!"

SCRIPTURE IN ACTION!

Do you realize how powerful that is? Just recently, we revisited the Maputo garbage dump. One of the workers on top of the mountain of garbage, a woman, was unhappy with happy praise songs and grew belligerent. I can tell when someone is not happy in any language!

I asked the translator, "What is she saying?"

"She's wondering why you are singing a song like that in a place like this!"

She could not make the connection. Indeed, how could we be so joyful in the very place in which she labored day after day, year after dismal year, foraging out a living from filthy, contaminated rubbish?

"I am so glad that you asked," I said, through the translator as I pulled out my little Bible. "Let me tell you why," and I read that little psalm to her. You should have seen her face change as she heard, "He lifts the poor from the dirt and the needy from the garbage dump...."

"Make sure you tell her that this was written long before she was here. She needs to hear and know that God has not forgotten her, that God has come right here today to visit her."

> *Make sure you tell her that this was written long before she was here.*

I explained to her, "You know, my heart wasn't any different. He came to the rubbish heap of my heart. Jesus found me and sovereignly picked me up and sent me out as a messenger of His joy!"

The very moment she heard the Gospel, she most willingly received the Lord Jesus Christ and His overwhelming love. Whoa, that was so much fun, and it was so easy. It takes effort and energy to get to these places, but once you are there, Jesus helps you find another trophy in the ash heap.

Bliss and Bubble Wrap

I am so completely satisfied with what Christ has done for me—the atonement, the work of the Cross; it is all so indescribable and beyond human reasoning. It is that unspeakable *joy*—the *wow*, the incredible bliss (ecstasy of salvation)—and He wants us to live in the joy and bliss factors *now* on this planet Earth. Why? So that we can show off who He is!

God wants to be acknowledged, to receive the glory due His name, and this comes by way of ecstatic saints walking in an "I'm so full," glory mindset. Listen, how can we ever reach the lost with an "I need, I need, I need," mindset? If the Lord is your Shepherd, you don't need a thing. (See Psalm 23 TM.) Open your mouth, and He shall fill it. The sky is filled with bread. Skies drop dews of wine. He nourishes you with honey from the cliffs, with olive oil from the hard rock.

Until He satisfies you, you will not know what satisfaction is. Religion can only offer junk food. You need to know the freedom you have to eat from the feast set upon the table. When the Lord feeds you, you lack nothing, nothing! His fresh pastures lead you to faith. Beside still waters, He converts your soul. It is all for His name's sake, for His glory. He brings you forth from desert lands, from empty, howling wastelands and dunghills—surrounding and watching over you as His most precious possession. (See Deuteronomy 32; Psalm 23.)

We live in a shadow of death because of what happened during the Fall. Nevertheless, we don't fear evil because He is in our midst, leading, guiding, living His life through us, even in this present shadow, even where you are right now.

Jesus says, "Daddy, don't take them out of the world; keep them here but keep them from the evil one." (See John 17:15.) You are covered in Holy Ghost bubble wrap. He wraps up His delicate, little, new creations and protects them from evil.

I Saw Two Tables

I had a vision recently of two tables, a rickety card table, the folding kind you bring from the closet when you have extra guests for dinner, and a very large, round table. It was so big no one would hear you say, "Hey, pass me the potatoes," and if they did hear you, they would need to FedEx them to you.

The Lord showed me that some of His people still feel as if they are eating from a little flimsy table that may collapse any second, and they are scared!

Is that you? Does it seem as if your enemies are breathing down your neck, about to steal your food away from you?

Which table are you sitting at? The Lord has prepared a sturdy table for us, and it is huge. Its grandeur is out of all proportion to the little rickety table, and it has been set in the wilderness right in front of your enemy. (See Second Samuel 17:27-29; Psalm 78:19.) It is so enormous that the enemy isn't even a consideration. Do you see the table and the riches He has provided? Do you see the Crucified One there? He gave us His body and said, "Eat!" He gave us His wine. Have you considered what is in that cup that He gave you to drink?

When Jesus was on the Cross, He was thirsty and asked for a drink. Collective humanity gave Him vinegar and gall. He drank that drink. So now, He gives you a cup. The wine is the blood that He shed for you, the blood that forgives your sin and washes you clean. He creates a new creation within when you believe that His body was given and His blood was poured out. He has prepared this table in your sight.

Is your mind happy, or is there something else going on there? Just change your diet and begin feasting at the table of the Lord. He is more than enough!

He fattens our heads with oil and gladdens our minds with spiritual joy. (See Psalms 23:5.)[1] It is at His table that we experience freedom to enjoy our salvation, freedom to express our joy at what He has done, and freedom to be satisfied!

The Bliss Realm—Reality!

You and I only have a few short years to know Him by faith and only a short time for that faith to become the substance that He desires. God is saying, "I need My saints to be out of their minds, to be caught up into divine ecstasy, to experience *wow*, now as they live on this earth." He has given you the faith to walk in this earth realm, and to connect the trail of dots as you go.

What nation burns on your heart? What people group? What garbage dump? Who has He given you to feed? Come and dine, come and feast, take more than you need so that it spills over into the ash heaps. There is more than enough wine in the cup, more than enough food on the table. Bread falls from Heaven. The wine cannot even stay in the cup. There's so much more than enough. (See Deuteronomy 33:28; Psalm 105:40 FBT.)

Endnote

1. NETBible notes on the King James Version: "anointest: Heb. makest fat"; http://net.bible.org/home.php; see also http://www.studylight.org/lex/heb/view.cgi?number= 01878; "dashen."

Part II

To the Outcast
on Her
Knees...Arise!

My lover spoke and said to me,
"Arise, my darling, my beautiful one, and come with me"
(Song of Solomon 2:10 NIV).

Are you feeling unstable in today's world? Shaken, discouraged, disappointed, anxious, or fearful? Take heart! Darkness is for His glory! Guaranteed, God will bring you through it. He is calling, "Come, come with Me, beautiful one! Arise!"

If you believe in Jesus and in His finished work, you walk in victory right now, in a spirit of expectancy and hope in His goodness, mercy, faithfulness, and grace! You can trust His promise to deliver you.

As our Part Two contributors know, there are overwhelming situations and circumstances, trials and challenges in our lives, but we must not let our feelings dictate how we seek or approach solutions. Rather, Sue, Sheri, and Nina have learned how to filter their feelings through the reality of Heaven—learning how God feels, sees, and thinks; getting vision and answers for their journeys; and living their destinies now by making demands on their faith and truly owning it.

May the God of the cosmos fill you with His peace as you join them on their journeys. May God, who knows your needs before you call His name, touch you with His tender mercies and love. And may you feel His presence in your spirit, mind, and body, and rise from your bed of defeat, sickness, depression, turmoil, and lack, for God is no respecter of persons or circumstances. He is able to deliver to the uttermost those who call upon His name.

Chapter 5

SOMEWHERE OUT THERE (WHERE DREAMS COME TRUE)

by Sue Ahn

Somewhere out there,
if love can see us through,
then we'll be together,
somewhere out there,
out where dreams come true.[1]

I learned rejection at a young age, shortly after our parents, both doctors, moved our family into a middle-class, all-white neighborhood in Cherry Hill, New Jersey. It was a difficult transition for a small child; I did not understand why the color of my skin meant I could not have friends. Being the new kid on the block is one thing, being the *Filipino* new kid is quite another.

For the first time in my life, I experienced what it was like to be sticks-and-stones different. At the school bus stop on the corner, children would hide behind bushes and hurl rocks at me. At noon, the peanut-butter-and-jelly crowd stayed far away from the girl with the dried fish, rice, and seaweed lunch, unless it was to toss an insult. *Hey, what's wrong? This fish is really good....* My little heart just did not understand why nobody liked me. I knew my parents loved me, and being raised Catholic, I was told that God loved me, so why was I still sitting alone with my lunch in the corner of the playground surrounded by piles of landed rocks?

I'd practice miracles with the rocks. "Jesus," I'd plead as I waved my hand over them, "please turn these into bread."

The stones remained stones day after day; the taunting remained as well; the hair pulling continued. I was fair game at recess tucked in my little corner away from the watchful eyes of the stern nuns.

One day, to escape the bullies, I left the playground and snuck into the nearby Catholic church, a huge building, and, in the stale darkness, prayed. Lonely and rejected, I was desperate to connect with God. *What am I good for?* Daily they taunted, and daily at recess I raced to the sanctuary, resolving to become a secluded nun as a way to communicate with God.

REALITY DISCONNECT

One morning I put my dime in the offering box, lit a candle, and prayed, "You owe me one, God. Ten cents worth of Your presence. That's all I'm asking, ten cents worth. Tomorrow, I'll give You a quarter."

It was how things worked in the Catholic church. I loved on Him in the way I'd learned to love on Him. My thinking was that I could earn His presence.

Suddenly, I heard singing, and I thought, *Oh no, the nuns are here...* *I'm busted.* I didn't want to look; the nuns who taught us were harsh, and in those days, corporal punishment was the norm. If they caught me... oh! I remained still—frozen with fear is more like it—expecting to be pulled up by the collar from where I knelt at any moment.

Over and over, they sang the same unfamiliar song. As I listened more intently, I realized I had never heard the nuns sing quite as beautifully. It was so strange!

The sisters never did show up, but God's presence did through my first, second, third, fourth, fifth grades—and all the way through! I have since come to realize that God, as I sought Him, had sent His angels to minister over me in a song of deliverance, removing the reality of rejection and the loneliness, and ushering in the *new reality* of the presence of the Lord.

> *God, as I sought Him, had sent His angels*
> *to minister over me in a song of deliverance.*

What is your reality? Loneliness as a single mother? A husband who doesn't quite get it and says he'll change, but doesn't? A wayward teen who has broken your heart? Discouragement? Rejection? The Lord is bringing songs of deliverance to you today. He is saying, "I am with you always. You will make it." Today I can rejoice that my rejection and loneliness drew me to God. One day, I pray, you will too.

Shifting Gears for Dream Breakthrough

God is with you, working the wheel, shaping the clay, and completing you in the fire. It is a *current* process. Your destiny is not out there somewhere; it is here and now. While it is true that with time, your destiny does take on a recognizable shape, your destiny was and is here, as mine was that day the angels sang over me in church, and as mine is right now.

Many of us tend to live in the destiny-future mindset, looking forward to that day when everything is clear, all systems are go, giftings are in place. Someone might give you a prophetic word, and you wait, wait for it to happen and wonder why it hasn't. All the while, you have been living your destiny but just have not realized it, and perhaps have even missed out on blessings—the thrill of life *now* in Christ, and the opportunity to glorify Christ—as a result.

Destiny seems to be the buzzword and catchall Kingdom phrase for hope and power to come, but it is hope and power *for today*. We wait for that accomplishment or opportunity and experience disappointment when it doesn't happen in the way we expected. As Anne Stock in her message will remind you, "Expect life not to be what you expect it." Good word, especially for mothers! I am a mother of four. I had them all in a row, like steps, all within 15-21 months of each other. Welcome to my world. Bam, one, two, three, four; I didn't get out of my pajamas for like ten years and homeschooled for fourteen years. It wasn't how I expected destiny to happen: days without a shower, kids with colds, snotty noses, mornings where I had to nuke my coffee four times in the microwave.... Throw one or two strong-willed children into the mix, and, well, you catch the drift. Certainly I had prophetic words over my life that looked a whole lot different but don't think for a moment that I was not living my destiny. It was there and then, and it is here and now.

> *It wasn't how I expected destiny to happen.*

ENGAGE THE SUPERNATURAL, NATURALLY

Many people live in church, never moving into the world to shine. We soak; we get healed up; we worship; we hang out with each other. That is all good stuff, but to whom are we witnessing? What are we waiting for? Are we afraid of destiny? Are we afraid to be who we are? It is all glory in church, but what happens when you go to work? Do you "hide?" Please don't be afraid of rejection. What I learned most when God healed me of rejection was that there will always be people who dislike me or what I stand for, there will always be those who misunderstand or who do not have the same passions, and that's OK. I take that to Him and just continue to trust in His presence with me in *and* out of church.

God desires us to be supernatural, naturally, with evangelism and our faith as natural outflows of our godly nature and God's presence within us. The best evangelistic method or faith tool I have is to ask God, "Please help me to be a good lover of people today; help me to love well whomever You place in my path, whether I'm at the gas station, or the bank, or the grocery store. Please, Holy Spirit, remind me to love well."

SAY GOOD-BYE TO RELIGIOSITY

In this way, I don't have to worry and wonder, "Oh, did I do it right, encourage her the right way, quote the right Scripture?" We call it "legalism," and being raised in the Catholic church, I do know that religiosity sets many up for failure and a critical spirit, which I had, especially while raising teens.

They wanted to do things that teens do—piercings, tattoos....

Whoa! "You will not pierce yourself *there,* young lady!" Of course, my daughter pulled the old, "Well, Jesus was pierced."

"Well, you just get up there on the Cross; you show me…*now* do you want a piercing?"

Religiosity, rules, and law kicked in, and at first I struggled with it. I was thinking *swine, nose ring, swine…* and *How will this make us look at church…the pastors' daughter with a big, honking nose ring?* The Lord showed me my errors, however, and said, "Don't judge; be grateful that she came to you. Go with her; understand her."

> *Religiosity can push our children and any loved one away.*

Religiosity can push our children and any loved one away. It can cause them to close their hearts. There were times, I know, when my teens' hearts, already just open a crack, slammed shut because of my legalistic criticism. This was not Christlike!

Keep fanning the love flame even when things don't look so good. God is doing stuff we are not even aware of, and the very thing we are critical of may be the exact thing He is using to transform someone— perhaps even shaping or testing them in the fire.

GET VISION

Julie Chrystyn, in her best-selling book *The Secret to Life Transformation: How to Claim Your Destiny Now!,* writes about how to create a vision for your life, and how to make that vision a reality. She should know. Julie grew up in communist Yugoslavia, persecuted and poor. As a twelve-year-old, four years after coming to America, she spent six months on her back in a full-body cast after surgery to repair a forty-five-degree spinal curve.

She could not lift her head, sit up, or lift her arms to even read a book; all she could do was look out the window, listen to the radio, or think. While there were medical ways to manage her physical suffering, nothing could ease her mental anguish. The reality of her future was frightful, severely limited. In her words, "The tragic fact of our reality is that our lives do not accurately reflect what we are capable of becoming."[2]

With nothing but time on her hands, she thought about her future, and mapped it out, determining not to accept any limitations and resolving to expect a full recovery. Realizing that she was well behind where she wanted to be one day, and desperate to transform her reality, she developed a plan for an "option-filled life."[3] Faith, which she describes as "precondition to resolution"[4] was necessary for the vision because it is the substance of things hoped for; it is "what you can see that others cannot."[5]

> *She developed a plan for an "option-filled life."*

Her results were miraculous as she activated herself to stop thinking about her limitations and discovered ways around them. Because of this transformation of her mind, she found a new freedom and empowerment to overcome obstacles and let nothing stop her.

THE POWER OF A TRANSFORMED MIND

Therefore, I urge you, brothers, in view of God's mercy, to offer your bodies as living sacrifices, holy and pleasing to God—this is your spiritual act of worship. Do not conform any longer to the pattern of this world, but be transformed by the renewing of your mind. Then you will be able to test and approve what God's will is—His good, pleasing and perfect will (Romans 12:1-2 NIV).

What is your reality? No matter what it may be, remember this: it is not the end for you. Look back on things you have accomplished that you never thought you could do, but did. That's the picture here. I am who I am today because I grew up rejected and determined not to let it become my reality. Did you grow up in poverty, and do you use that as an excuse why you cannot land the job of your dreams? You can choose the clichéd life-half-empty as an excuse or determine to live a filled and overflowing life, beautiful woman of God!

The transformed mind is one that shifts from one's own thinking, to God's thinking. God does not have a poverty or victim mindset. His is a big, oh yes, very big mind. It is holy, gracious, accepting, loving, extravagant, creative, abundant, and without time constraints. Now wouldn't it be beautiful if we could always think in those godly ways?

I encourage you: do whatever it takes to have His mind. I remember when I was raising the children how I'd race to the washroom to spend time with Jesus in prayer and in the Word. Seriously, the children would be banging on the door asking for Cheerios, and I'd be sitting on the closed potty with my Bible: "Like, wake me up from all this, Lord…!"

Today we have iPods that we can load with worship music or the Word, and just ignore the noise, hallelujah. Whatever it takes, my friends, renew your mind and transform your reality.

Transforming is a constant replenishing, just as the cells in our bodies are constantly renewing in every part of us. This might take some altering of our lifestyles because often we are comfortable in our reality, in what we already know, as the Israelites were. They had the promise of a land of milk and honey, but some chose to remain where they were.

FILTER YOUR REALITY

Be able to filter life through your belief system, and your belief system should come about by the discovery of knowing who you are and why you are here through a personal one-on-one relationship with God. The more time we spend with Him; the more like Him we become.

Knowledge of the Lord's and my own identity was spoon-fed to me while I was growing up. The church told me what God was and what He was not, and what sin was—and, oh my gosh, I was going to hell because I didn't give up my chewing gum for Lent. "I'm sorry, God, I failed." I felt as if I had murdered someone, doomed to purgatory with the people who murdered all the first-century Christians.

> *"I'm sorry, God, I failed."*

"Chill out," says the Holy Spirit, "It's only gum."

INQUIRE

We do not know who we are because we do not inquire of the Lord. Jesus did, and He grew in wisdom, stature, and favor with God and with man. David inquired of the Lord, sought Him out, and he became King of Israel, forever known as the man after God's own heart. Even when he greatly sinned, he could approach God because he knew Him as a loving and merciful Father.

God wants you to deal with and settle the question of who you are and why you are here because in so doing, you will be living your destiny *now.* As you gain clarity, you will discover that you don't have to compete with another living soul, prove anything, strive for something, or try to create something by your own strength. You won't have to worry that your skin is another color or that people won't like you. Even if they throw stones at you, it won't matter because you are secure. You won't have to feel as if you have to be like anyone else because you are uniquely created and gifted in Him. You will know that you are where you need to be in this world. You will not feel the need to be judgmental or critical of others as a result.

> God wants you to deal with and settle
> the question of who you are
> and why you are here.

I have sensed a growing assault on covenantal relationships: marriage, sisterhood, friendship, brotherhood. Church unity is a mess, and divorce is on the rise. The power of a transformed mind, choosing God's way of thinking, can change the reality of a bad marriage. The reality of your future together may appear limited or impossible, but that reality does not accurately reflect what it is capable of becoming. Again, it is a question of choice not to accept the reality, resolving instead to expect a full recovery. This comes about by thinking as God thinks, surrendering your reality, and developing a plan by faith to transform it, even if the other person cannot see what you can see. How does God think? Unconditional, extravagant love and forgiveness. Inquire of the Holy Spirit, "What do You want for us?" He will not barge in or intrude. He is your Counselor and Advisor, so instead of fretting, fighting, or trying to repair the breach in your relationship, choose to turn to Him. This is, in itself, the actual turning or transformation of the mind: the choice to go to Him for that counseling.

He surely was my Counselor as a little Catholic school girl in Cherry Hill...and ten years into my marriage, but the latter is another story.

Release control and surrender. Surrender's process brings you to that place of being able to say, "Wow, I don't have to have it all together or know all the answers."

MAKE DEMANDS ON YOUR FAITH

We also live our destiny now by making demands on our faith and truly owning it. If you truly believe it, you will achieve it.

After our son Gabriel was born, he was sickly and quiet; he hardly ate and wasn't gaining weight. His skin had a yellow hue, and something just wasn't right.

"This is the worst case of jaundice I have ever seen," said the doctor. "Get him to Holy Cross Hospital right away!"

Jaundice that severe can cause death because it can lead to blood poisoning, affecting the brain and major organs. Gabriel, at that juncture, was dying.

> *Gabriel, at that juncture, was dying.*

At the hospital they decided to fly in a specialist from a large children's hospital, and immediately upon his arrival, he wanted to give Gabriel a blood transfusion. He would also need a spinal tap and liver sample; they also discovered a hole in his heart.

The blood transfusion needle was huge, and as it neared him, I yelled, "Stop!" This blood purification procedure at the time was quite new, experimental, and scary. My husband had not yet arrived; we needed to pray about this, needed some wisdom. It was all happening too fast, and something just did not *feel* right. Here was this promised child of God, prophesied over before he was born, and his life was not as I expected it to be. "Lord, You will have to give me a word because I dedicated this child to You while he was yet in the womb, prayed over him, and prophesied into his life. Three times a day we prayed that he would walk with You all the days of his life, and that if he's called to be married, You would find his right life partner."

Che, my husband, showed up distraught, as we both were. "Lord," we prayed, "take him if You want. We have willingly given You this child. If this is it, if we are to only have him for two weeks, so be it, but don't let him suffer."

"Life," replied the Lord to us both, "is in the blood."

Life is in the blood! It was the word we needed.

"We don't want him to have the transfusion," we told the doctor, who looked at us as though we were crazy.[6] "Why not try the special lights to reduce the bilirubin, as you usually treat jaundice in infants?"

"He needs more," the doctor insisted, "your son is well past that stage."

"Please try."

They acquiesced and placed him under the lights. Although we couldn't hold him, we prayed over him, and sang or played songs of deliverance. Within the first seven hours, to their surprise (but to our "Yea, God!"), Gabriel's bilirubin level dropped considerably, and eventually to normal. Moreover, within three months, the hole in his heart closed, and his healings became a powerful witness to the medical team at the hospital.

The doctors could only give us "at best" options.

Had I not sought and exercised wisdom, called upon the Lord, thought like Him to know His perfect will for the situation, seen the higher reality, who knows? The doctors could only give us "at best" options. At best, he will live. If he lives, at best, he'll be mentally retarded. Listen, because I put demands on my faith, I could say, "I don't think so! I respect you as doctors and your levels of expertise—hey, my parents are doctors—but I believe there is a better way because God told me so, and because God told me so, I believe for the best outcome for Gabriel, period. No *'at bests'* for us."

Don't Give Up

I graduated from George Washington University with a double major in special education. Special Education was new back then, a real step forward for humanity from the backward and cruel practice of placing the deaf, blind, crippled, and mentally ill or compromised children in asylums. The new way would be to provide a special education program that would eventually mainstream special needs children into regular classroom environments.

Before deciding on that major, I wasn't quite sure what I wanted to go into. At first I though about the arts, but then realized that such a career would not pay the bills; then I considered psychology—you know, to figure out the people who rejected me and perhaps help them. When this new program was introduced, I thought, *cool,* because it would include courses in both art therapy and psychology.

After four years at the university, I was excited to teach and make a difference in young lives. Convinced it was where God wanted me to be, I sent out thirty-two smashing, full-color résumés. Thirty-two rejections later, I was disheartened but still determined; I sent out more. The thirty-third résumé yielded results: "We have a pilot classroom just starting, one of only a few in the area; it would just be a test period of about nine months, but if it works out, it might lead to a permanent position. Would you like the job?"

Would I!

However, when I met my students, I wondered whether I could handle it. The class comprised seven hard cases—all boys, all with deep challenges: schizophrenia, ADD, bipolar, and difficult pasts. One boy of seven would come to school with makeup on and draw faces on his stomach, pretending he was pregnant. His story? He witnessed his father commit suicide on the couch. Another little boy had unusual strength and would pick up desks and hurl them across the room in demonic-like furious outbursts.

The class comprised seven hard cases—all boys, all with deep challenges.

This was a time when I had to transform my mind from wanting to quit and believing I couldn't handle it or make headway to "I am called to be a special education teacher, called to this next generation. I will call upon the Holy Spirit, think as God thinks, and make a difference in these kids' lives."

Lo and behold, at the end of the testing period and during evaluations, every one of my students had excelled and would be streamlined into regular classrooms the following year. Moreover, I invited them to our wedding, and, oh wow, to see those little guys in their suits beaming up at me. Priceless.

"Lord," I said, "I present these ones to You, these ones who would have been *who knows where* if in the hands of another person or another place. Thank You that I had the ability and the honor of caring for them.

You put them in my hands, and I took those little fish and loaves, and multiplied them for Your glory because it was all I had."

You may be looking in your hands and thinking you do not have anything to offer God. You don't know your destiny; you are unsure of your calling; you don't know who you are or why you are here, but God is pointing to your hands and saying, "Your destiny is there." Put it all there! Give what you have and ask Him to bless it and multiply it to bless others. In the end, it is not about us at all; it is everything about God.

As you learn to think as God thinks, you will have the wisdom to accomplish the impossible. By placing demands on your faith, you can walk right into your calling. In living your destiny now, you are living to glorify Him now. When you know who you are and why you are here, you will know how He defines you. As you spend time together with your Creator, you will know your purpose and walk in it—free of religious constraints and equipped to transform the world for His glory.

At the very least, sticks and stones may break your bones, but names will *never* hurt you. That, beautiful one, is beautiful!

PRAYER

Father, I thank You that we can call You "Father." I thank You that You call us Your "children," and I thank You that You love us with everlasting, unending love. I pray that each one of us would embrace wherever we may be in life, that we would find You, not just to try to solve a problem, but to find You in the problem, in the storm, in the transition, in the process. We release and surrender to You right now all expectations, questions, every hindering religious paradigm, any fear, negative mindset, critical spirit, or thought of rejection that prevents us from completing what You want to do within each of our lives. We submit ourselves to You, and say, "Thy will be done, Thy Kingdom come right here, right now, and into each of our lives," in Jesus' name, Amen!

ENDNOTES

1. "Somewhere Out There," from *An American Tale*. Lyricist: Cynthia Weil; composers James Horner and Barry Mann.

2. Julie Chrystyn, *The Secret to Life Transformation: How to Claim Your Destiny Now!* (Beverly Hills, CA: Dove Books, 2009), 207.

3. Chrystyn, 209.

4. Chyrstyn, 210.

5. Ibid.

6. Let me caution you, unless you clearly hear from the Lord to the contrary, do not forego needed medicine or surgical procedures. God works His miracles in many ways, including through doctors and medicine. This was a specific instance in which we were completely confident based on what we already knew to be true, and, we were not foregoing medical intervention, simply suggesting something else, first. Wisdom, wisdom, wisdom in all things.

Chapter 6

WHEN THE BOTTOM DROPS OUT OF YOUR WORLD

by Sheri Hess[1]

It took us all by surprise.

In a wild flurry of events, our seemingly "normal" life came to an abrupt halt that Thanksgiving week of 1997. Within moments we found ourselves sobered by the realities of life and death.

My husband, David, and I had been pastoring our church for a number of years. It was a wonderful experience. Our children—Bethany, age 16, Ben, age 12, and Brandon, age 9—were right beside us in the middle of it all. We saw many people turn to Jesus. We watched the Father's love heal wounded hearts and restore wounded bodies. We grew, shared life with one another, and enjoyed the presence of the Lord together. It felt like the life we were created to live.

But one cold November evening, everything seemed to change. David had been feeling tired for some time. When I would cast a troubled glance in his direction, he told me not to worry, promising he would slow down soon. *Right*, I thought, *I've heard that before.* I tried not to nag about going to see a doctor, but his body soon betrayed symptoms which left us with no choice. Strange bruises began to appear; the whites of his eyes turned to a yellowish shade; his gums started to bleed; and black sores covered the inside of his mouth.

*I tried not to nag about going to see a doctor,
but his body soon betrayed symptoms
which left us with no choice.*

With his reluctant approval, we went to the doctor.

By evening the blood tests revealed the worst.

David had leukemia. It was acute myeloid leukemia, to be exact—the worst strain of this deadly disease. "Most people," we were told, "do not survive this aggressive, cancerous attack on the immune system."

Shortly after we arrived at the cancer ward of a local hospital the next morning, one of the nurses echoed this ominous report. "He may not live to see Christmas," she said with a trembling voice, tearful pools filling her eyes.

Now What?

What do you do when you feel like the bottom has dropped out of your life?

I was raised to think positively and believe for the best. Like the popular song from the 1970s (during my early days in Jesus) says, I had signed up for "happiness all the time." Jesus did miracles—lots of them! With my own eyes, I had witnessed Him working wonders in many lives spanning our ministry years. We prayed, and God moved.

But here I was, praying fervently for David—alongside our whole church body which had enlisted in the cause—yet nothing seemed to happen.

Not being one to take life lying down, I shifted between two mindsets.

First, the warrior's heart arose within me. Armed with weapons of faith and compassion, I cried out to my Father. We "have not" because we "ask not" (see James 4:2), so I asked. "Father, heal my David. You are bigger than cancer. You conquered leukemia on the Cross. Bring Your victory into his body and Your strength into his weakness." On I went, roaring and warring.

And then, the prophet's heart stood beside the warrior. The question I heard in my spirit was, *What is God saying?* I needed to hear His voice. I had listened to the voices of the medical community, and other opinions were being stuffed daily into the suggestion box. With so many perspectives swirling, I became desperate to hear what my Father had to say.

As the seriousness of the situation overwhelmed my mind, I had to face the thought, *What if this is David's "time"?* I heard myself professing, "David is Yours, Lord. He always has been. We have had nineteen wonderful years together. And we have three great kids. I didn't think this would end so soon, but if You want to take him, He's Yours."

"But I'm not ready to give him up so quickly!"

Then the warrior's growl turned into a full roar, and I heard myself cry out: "If it *is* his 'time,' he is not leaving this earth because of some *sick disease!* He will leave it well. Whole. Complete!"

God did not send this sickness. As our friend Bill Johnson often quips, "God is good. The devil is bad." God doesn't send diseases to teach His children. He sends the Holy Spirit to do that, who teaches us "all things." (See John 14:26.) Circumstances are merely the backdrop to His instruction. He teaches us His ways, revealing His secrets in spite of the attacks. Even if the devil throws his worst at us, the School of the Holy Spirit never closes.

There, in that moment, I shifted into "war mode." From the place of resting in His presence, I stood on His promises and received a life-changing revelation of His heart which penetrated a new level in my own heart.

> *There in that moment,*
> *I shifted into "war mode."*

I was learning that even in the toughest situations, God is faithful. He showed me His posture in our trials: He comes as a *"very present help"* in a time of trouble (see Ps. 46:1). "Very present" is better than merely being present. It speaks of a God who steps in *before* the trial strikes. His help is in place even before we need it!

I began experiencing a level of His manifest presence that knocked the fear right out of me. His peace was bypassing my brain—sidestepping my understanding. I am increasingly convinced, in the hour in which we live, that God wants each of us to experience extreme levels of the depth of His love, the comfort of His nearness, and the peace of His presence.

As we prayed—and waited—we heard God's voice. His truth came, setting us free from fear. This would be a fierce battle, but we would win!

TIMELY WORDS

One way we heard our Father's voice and received His truth was through Scripture. Verses spoken over us "in season" sprouted to life and sustained us during dark hours.

One afternoon, we heard delicate footsteps coming down the tiled hospital hallway and into David's room. Mary's meager thirteen years of age belied her bravery. With a faith and courage outstripping her petite stature, she had fought ovarian cancer—and won.

Mary stood with her mother beside David's bed and shared her story. She spoke of how the Lord had comforted her in the middle of her storm. He gave her a Scripture, which she wrote on a small note card and hung beside her bed. Those words daily ministered strength, hope, and healing:

> I will not die but live, and will proclaim what the Lord has done (Psalm 118:17 NIV).

As she passed the card to David, he held it firmly, meditated on it for a while, and then posted it on his wall. Like glue to our spirits, this word stuck! It ignited us with fresh faith and fire to overcome this battle. Amazingly, in that day's mail we received five other cards with the same Scripture written inside.

A few weeks later, as David was recovering from a difficult round of chemotherapy, he received another timely Scripture. Restless in his hospital-issued gown and rubber mattress, he sat up in his bed in the middle of the night. All was quiet. In the midst of that stillness, he heard a faint voice whispering a Scripture reference. *"Nahum 1:9. Nahum 1:9,"* it said, over and over.

> *In the midst of that stillness,*
> *he heard a faint voice*
> *whispering a Scripture reference.*

Puzzled, David grabbed his Bible and focused his eyes in the dim light to read: "…this affliction will not return a second time."

The next morning, David excitedly shared the incident with me. Only minutes later, one of his physicians stopped by to give us an update. "You're doing better than we expected. Your body is responding, and your immune system is getting stronger. But I don't want you to get your hopes up," he cautioned. "Often leukemia comes back a *second time*, with a vengeance."

Those words could have been devastating. But after he left the room, we chose instead to declare the Word of the Lord: "It will not return a second time!" And we got our hopes up!

In addition to His written Word, the Lord gave us prophetic words as weapons of war. Some were spoken years before David became ill. To be honest, at the time we received them, they offered no immediate meaning. But we held onto them, anyway.

One time we had been at a Rick Joyner conference when, during a fifteen-minute session with a small prophetic ministry team, the word of the Lord to us came something like this: "You will walk down a very dark corridor. But satan is about to make a grave tactical error. What he intends to use to destroy you will in fact release you into a greater place of faith. When you come out on the other side, you will strengthen and help many people."

In addition, prophetic teacher Cindy Jacobs had shared with David that he would go to Tibet and set many people free. But David had never been to Tibet. (And, when he got out of this situation, I wasn't about to let him go there for a while!) So we assumed the Lord had plans for David which were yet to be fulfilled.

But more than the words spoken by others, I was powerfully ministered to by the personal voice of my Shepherd speaking directly to my spirit. He continually whispered, *He will live. David will live. He will not die. He will tell what I have done.* Often I would turn on the radio, and a timely song would be playing. I would hear the familiar strains of a hymn like *Great Is Thy Faithfulness*, or Twila Paris' voice assuring me, "God is in control. We believe that His children will not be forsaken...."

Times of refreshing do come from His presence!

It is so important to hear God's voice.

His voice is truth.

And truth is God's version of reality.

Higher Truth

I was learning that there are different levels of truth. This was a hard concept for me to grasp, since I have a strong, prophetic temperament. I see things as clear-cut: either something is true, or it isn't true. Take your pick, but you can't have it both ways.

But the Father was showing me another way. I believed God, and I believed that His words to me were true. Now, as the group Petra sings, He was taking me "Beyond Belief."

You see, it's true that each of us have sinned. But it is *more true* that we have been forgiven. When you get stuck on the first truth (*I'm a sinner*), you never move on to the higher truth (*I'm a forgiven daughter! An accepted son!*). Proverbs 23:7 tells us, *"As a man thinks in his own heart, so is he."* We live out of who we think we are. That means it's possible for us to get stuck at one level of truth, and never move on to higher truth.

So while it's true that we have been forgiven, it's *more true* that we have a calling—a significant role to play in the Kingdom. What happens when we focus on what we have been *released from* but fail to get in touch with what we've been *released to?* Though we'll certainly be rewarded with Heaven when we die, we'll miss walking in victory while we're here.

As the Holy Spirit instructed me, I was continually reminded of His perspective: *it is true* that David has leukemia, but it is *more true* that God said he will not die but live to tell the story!

ENDURING THE CONTRADICTION

Even after acknowledging God's higher truth, our battle was not over. I engaged in continual skirmishes of the mind to remain in a place of trust. Holding that ground became increasingly difficult as the doctors' reports seemed to shout the opposite reality. Our truth was in conflict with what *appeared* to be true. I heard Lance Wallnau say, "When God makes a promise and the circumstances challenge that promise, hold fast to what God has said. Learn to *endure the contradiction.*"

I was enduring the contradiction. And ladies, it was harder than enduring contractions! I daily labored to *"hold fast the confession of our hope"* (Heb. 10:23), but I was becoming weary.

That's when fatigue set in. Each morning I was getting the kids off to school and then rushing over to spend a few hours with David. There by his hospital bed, I tried to keep him informed about family matters, pay the bills, answer letters, and make phone calls. By mid-afternoon I'd rush home to greet the children as they got off the bus, with homework beginning immediately. Many caring friends delivered a wide variety of casseroles during those days. If there was an hour left after homework and dinner, we would take a quick trip to the hospital for the kids to see their dad. We'd fly home to bed, and the routine began again in a few hours. Though we survived months of this frantic routine, I was spent.

David's hair had fallen out, and I was about to pull mine out.

Just as the serpent harassed Eve with his "did God *really* say?" taunts, the accuser of the brothers and sisters was terrorizing me:

You don't pray enough. Or do enough. If you were smarter, you would know which Scriptures to quote to make this go away. Maybe all of this is your fault. You're responsible to make the right choice. Maybe you haven't made the right choices.

On top of these internal naggings, some people were leaving our church, accusing us of not having enough faith. *If we really believed in healing, why did David receive chemotherapy? Why didn't we "just trust God"?*

As all of these pressures and confusions converged, I began to feel very alone.

THE FEAR FACTOR

Fear attacked me. It used intimidation to bully me into feeling small, insignificant, and unprotected. Because of fear, ten spies saw themselves as "grasshoppers," and were unable to enter the land promised to them. Fear tried to keep me from entering into the Father's promises, too.

Suddenly I was afraid to drive. And as incredible as it sounds, I was afraid to walk through a shopping mall! Without David by my side, I felt vulnerable and uncovered.

Without David by my side,
I felt vulnerable and uncovered.

It was during this time that a man in our neighborhood became emotionally unglued. Frequently he ended his day by screaming at his wife and children, threatening to kill himself. He would storm out of his house into the back yard, firing his gun into the air. On those nights I would stare at the ceiling, praying for the shooting to end and the morning to come. I prayed for my children. Then I prayed even more fervently for David to come home.

The church bought us a cell phone. Since the model was circa 1997, it matched the dimensions of a size eight sneaker! Yet I carried that phone everywhere, clutching it like it was my only connection to safety.

Someone had given me a one hundred dollar bill as a gift. I tucked it in my wallet for security—"just in case." Finally I realized something: I was beginning to lean on things, rather than on Jesus. Fear had crafted an insidious plan to separate my heart from God's heart.

And yes, the age-old question of "why" badgered me. David seemed to have a grace on him because I never heard him ask, "Why?" nor did I see him lash out in anger or frustration against God. That frustrated me even more! The longer this ordeal extended, the more agitated I became.

I was coming to the end of my strength, and I knew it.

FAITH TO CLIMB MOUNTAINS

That's when God's strength began to kick in.

I remember crying out to Him: *My faith is so small—maybe even smaller than a mustard seed. I need more. Help me to believe You. Help me to trust You more!*

Just as Jesus gives us *His* peace, fills us with *His* love and gives us the gift of *His* righteousness—He also offers us *His* quality of faith. He said, *"Have faith in God"* (Mark 11:22b). Many Bible scholars have translated this: "Have the faith *of* God" or "Have the kind of faith that *comes from God.*"

And that's what He did for me. It didn't happen in one monumental encounter or lightning strike from God. Instead I witnessed a sure, steady increase of His strength in my life. Tim Spirk, our dear friend and worship pastor at our church, said to me, "Sometimes He gives us the faith to move mountains. At other times, He gives us the faith to climb them."

> *Sometimes He gives us the faith*
> *to move mountains.*
> *At other times, He gives us*
> *the faith to climb them.*

THE HELP OF HIS PRESENCE

Psalm 42:5 records this powerful statement:

Why are you in despair, O my soul? And why have you become disturbed within me? Hope in God, for I shall again praise Him for the help of His presence (Psalm 42:5 NASB).

There are so many ways the Lord helped me. But the greatest help was "the help of His presence." He relentlessly pursued me, overwhelming me time and time again with His nearness and His peace.

Sometimes the way He revealed His proximity seemed unusual. Most days I had the physical sensation that I was wearing a hat. As I pondered this, I realized it served as a tangible reminder of the Lord's presence. It brought peace to the battle in my mind and squelched the lie of feeling uncovered. It was as if His "helmet of salvation" was being placed upon me. Randy Clark told me of others who experienced the same phenomenon. He said such a feeling is often the sign of "angelic presence." Angels who come as ministering spirits have also been called "flames of fire." (See Hebrews 1:7.) It may very well have been a sign of angelic presence in the upper room when flames of fire rested on the heads of the one hundred and twenty gathered there.

Our next door neighbor, a dear believer in Jesus, told me she sensed there were angels stationed around our property.

His presence was near me.

His angels were surrounding me.

His peace was guarding me.

A FINAL BLOW

The cancer unit had been David's home for a wearying five months, but now spring was returning. As I left for the hospital in the morning, the birds were singing and chirping in conversation. As the sun graced us with longer evenings, I found myself pacing the soccer field sidelines, cheering on my sons (loudly—as they would tell you!).

These changes were a welcome reprieve.

But then the phone call came.

It was one of David's nurses: *Mrs. Hess, you must come to the hospital right away. Your husband's appendix has ruptured, and we can't operate on him.*

David had just completed his final round of chemotherapy. As a result, his blood had minimal levels of platelets (blood-clotting agents) and white cells (infection-fighting agents). In plain words, his body was inoperable, and now filled with toxic fluid.

A doctor greeted me as I rushed toward David's room. Her face was grave. "We've done all that we could for him. There's nothing else to be done. I'm so sorry," she said softly, fighting back the tears. "He was such a nice guy. We'll do everything we can to make him comfortable."

I heard what they were saying. *David is going to die.*

That was the message, based on the facts. Yet being poured upon me at the same moment was incredible peace. It was a "beyond my understanding" peace.

> *I slept surrounded in the peace of my Father's arms, knowing that David was in His hands.*

So I walked into David's room, kissed him on his hairless head, prayed for him…and then went home.

I fell into a deep sleep. I slept surrounded in the peace of my Father's arms, knowing that David was in His hands—and I was, too.

David lived for six-and-a-half weeks with a burst appendix inside him. The medical staff was baffled, since people can only survive a few days after such an occurrence. Every day was a miracle, and every day they checked his blood levels, awaiting the time they could attempt an operation.

On the day he was finally cleared for surgery, there was a peace from God guarding my heart and keeping my mind.

Following David's procedure, we were surprised to learn from the surgeon that David's appendix had been encased by a "pouch" that had formed around his appendix—prior to its rupturing. All the toxic fluids were contained in this supernatural pouch. He suffered no internal damage whatsoever.

Within a few days, I escorted David out of the hospital, appendix-free.

And cancer-free.

Fresh Perspectives

This entire ordeal was anything but fun. I'm so grateful that God gave us the words that David would not die, and this affliction would not return a second time. But more than anything else, my life has been forever changed by the realization of the overwhelming closeness of God's presence.

No matter what you are walking through, I declare over you the words of Corrie ten Boom: "No pit is so deep that He is not deeper still."

Why did all of this happen to our family? I still don't know.

I'm learning to live with mystery and to trust, even when I don't understand. In my darkest moments, I wanted a formula, but I found a Father.

I do know that God did not cause this disease to come.

Rather, He makes all things work together for good in the lives of those who love Him (see Rom. 8:28). The "things" we walk through—the good, the bad, and the ugly—are all part of "all things." He is able to take things intended for evil and redeem them for His purposes.

As I reflect on these events, I realize several powerful things happened to us:

> *We had the opportunity to see our hearts at a deeper level.*

Circumstances have a way of exposing what we are truly leaning on and trusting in. David and I are both first-borns. We're prone to want to do everything right and can be driven and performance-oriented if we're not watchful.

During this season we realized that life is not about our perfect performance. Instead, our hearts needed to be reestablished in our Father's love. We became more deeply "rooted and grounded" in His affections.

We learned that trusting in God involves swimming farther out in the ocean than simply "believing in Him." We never had the opportunity to trust Him at this level before. But through that year, we developed a whole-hearted confidence, where we could trust even when we didn't understand. We trust Him because we know He's in control. He goes before us, removing obstacles from our path.

> *Trusting in God involves swimming*
> *farther out in the ocean*
> *than simply "believing in Him."*

Do you remember the one hundred dollar bill I had safely hidden in my wallet—my "security" deposit? Shortly after David was healed and back home, the Lord gave me a "foundation check." He wanted to show me what was really going on in my heart, and how He had changed me. When the Lord brings revelation, He is not primarily looking for dirt. Rather, He's searching to uncover treasure.

As David and I were visiting a missionary couple one day, the Lord whispered to me, "Give them the one hundred dollar bill." Without thinking twice, I handed the bill to the wife.

She needed it. That bill spoke to her of the Lord's devotion and dedication to provide for them.

And I needed to give it. That simple gesture revealed the intricacies of my heart. I was truly learning to put my trust in God's ability, not my own.

> *We saw the Lord (and experienced Him)*
> *in ways we never had before.*

Jewelers have found that diamonds will best display the exquisite beauty of every facet when presented on a black velvet backdrop. During our "dark time" we were able to see multiple facets of the nature of God. We certainly knew about these dimensions but had never experienced them with such intensity.

> *Diamonds will best display*
> *the exquisite beauty of every facet*
> *when presented on a black velvet backdrop.*

His ever-present help was constant and refreshing. We encountered Him as Healer. Our amazing Provider. The One who gives strength to our weakest places. A Refuge. A Shelter. A Fortress in the fiercest battles.

The One who draws near.

And never leaves.

> *We walked through doors of opportunity*
> *to touch the lives of others.*

Second Corinthians 1:4 says God *"comforts us in all our troubles, so that we can comfort those in any trouble with the comfort we ourselves have received from God."* (NIV) We soon realized we were fighting this fight, not just for ourselves, but for many others encountering similar attacks.

My husband never saw himself as an author. But several years ago, the Lord stirred David to share his journey in a book—a book that could go places where we would never travel and touch people we would never meet. Since the release of *Hope Beyond Reason*, we have been amazed by accounts of those who have been saved, healed, and touched by God's love as they read it. We can echo the words of Paul: *"...what has happened to me has really served to advance the gospel"* (Phil. 1:12 NIV).

Since the time of his healing in the summer of 1998, David has been cancer-free. Acute leukemia surrendered to Almighty God.

One of the questions most frequently asked of me is the following: "What if David had died? What would you have done then?"

During those long, difficult days as we battled for David's life, I felt the strong presence of the Lord. I can't fully explain it, but I know that whatever the outcome, the Lord would have been there for me!

> *"What if David had died?*
> *What would you have done then?"*

In one of the fiercest seasons, David asked us to publicly read Philippians 1:19-28 to the church. I will never forget the impact that passage had on our church family. These words continue to stir me today:

For I know that through your prayers and the help given by the Spirit of Jesus Christ, what has happened to me will turn out for my deliverance. I eagerly expect and hope that I will in no way be ashamed, but will have sufficient courage so that now as always Christ will be exalted in my body, whether by life or by death. For to me, to live is Christ and to die is gain. If I am to go on living in the body, this will mean fruitful labor for me. Yet what shall I choose? I do not know! I am torn between the two: I desire to depart and be with Christ, which is better by far; but it is more necessary for you that I remain in the body. Convinced of this, I know that I will remain, and I will continue with all of you for your progress and joy in the faith, so that through my being with you again your joy in Christ Jesus will overflow on account of me. Whatever happens, conduct yourselves in a manner worthy of the gospel of Christ. Then, whether I come and see you or only hear about you in my absence, I will know that you stand firm in one spirit, contending as one man for the faith of the gospel without being frightened in any way by those who oppose you (Philippians 1:19-28 NIV).

Beautiful one, God wants you to know the strength of His presence. Right now you may feel that, in yourself, you are not strong enough to face your challenges. You may be sighing, "I am weak." And that may be true.

But there is a higher truth: in Him, you are strong!

You are *"strong in the Lord and in the strength of His might!"* (Eph. 6:10 NASB).

You may have a "little seed" of faith, but with that seed, you have access to Him. You have access to His faith and all the resources of Heaven.

In closing, I would like to pray my personal paraphrase of Ephesians 3:16-21 over you:

I pray that He, the Father of our Lord Jesus Christ, would grant you, out of His glorious riches, to be strengthened with power through His Spirit in your inner being—so that Christ may dwell in your heart through faith. And I also pray that you, being rooted and established in love, may have power together with all the saints to grasp (to wrap your brain around) how high, how deep, how wide, how long is the love of Christ. I pray that you would know this love. That you would experience this love that surpasses knowledge so that you may be filled, filled, filled—and filled again—to the measure of the fullness of God!

I believe as you receive these words of truth, which are God's version of reality, He will pour out upon you in extreme measure…

His strength,

His love,

His presence,

And His peace.

ENDNOTE

1. Editor's Note: Special thanks and blessings to David Hess for his assistance with the editing of Sheri's message, a testimony of courage and God's faithfulness, which truly belongs to them both.

Chapter 7

STUCK IN A BAD PLACE?
FIND YOUR FOCUS

by Sue Ahn

"Jesus! J-e-s-u-s! *Jesus!*" screamed a boy in our Sunday school while peering down the neck of his shirt.

"OK, Tommy," I said, thinking he was, you know, using the Lord's name in vain or something. "*What* is going on here?"

"Well, Pastor Sue, *you* said that Jesus heals, and *you* said that He lives in my heart, and I am still not healed!"

"Go on…."

"Well, I just didn't think that He could hear me, so I'm yelling real loud."

Yelling at his heart, where Jesus lives, of course!

Jesus honors that kind of tenacity, desperation, and diligence, especially in transition, when we are on the verge of something great but are not sure how it will look—in Tommy's case, a healing. As children's pastor at our church, Harvest Rock, it is a joy to be with these little giants who are so supernaturally natural and matter-of-fact.

Before worship we have "Say So" time, and the children can't wait to come up and declare, "Jesus say so, my boo-boo's healed." God sees that faithfulness!

Hey, good news, you're going to make it to "Say So" time too!

Find Your Focus

We do not always understand healing, but the idea is not to focus on the problem; the idea is to find God. If it takes yelling at your heart while looking down your shirt, go for it! He will never leave you empty-handed or empty-hearted as a result.

Focused vision is powerful, even more so when the vision is God. *"My eyes are focused on You, O Sovereign Lord; in You I take refuge—do not give me over to death"* (Ps. 141:8.) It becomes a refuge. Without such vision, people perish (see Prov. 29:18 KJV).

> *He will never leave you*
> *empty-handed or empty-hearted.*

The right focus can mean incredible power to you. Let me give you an example. On sunny days, my brother used to burn bugs or worms (yuck, forgive him, Father) through a magnifying glass. He would angle the lens so that it caught the sun, which by the way is around 55,000 degrees Celsius, and magnify its rays through it, concentrating the sun's energy into a single point. That focused stream of sunlight had amazing power.

Focusing on God yields much greater power. It was power enough to heal our marriage and obliterate the annoying pests that threatened it.

Shortly after my marriage to my husband, Che, the cute Asian pastor, he announced, "I think you have a spirit of fear."

Through no fault of his own, I had developed weird fears, such as being alone. He had to travel to South Africa for three weeks, and while he was gone I put fourteen locks on the door. At some point, I also developed a fear of germs and washed my hands all the time.

> *Through no fault of his own,*
> *I had developed weird fears,*
> *such as being alone.*

"Aren't you afraid of germs, too?" I asked. (Wasn't everyone?)

He shook his head. "It's not normal, darling."

Peacefully and wonderfully he said, "Just ask the Holy Spirit."

Then he counseled me to renounce the spirit of fear in Jesus' name. I didn't even know what "renounce" meant, so he led me through deliverance.

The focus was on Jesus, who did not want me to live in fear and torment. That night was the beginning of the power of the spirit of love and a sound mind in my life, and I slept like a baby, glory to God (see 2 Tim. 1:7).

WHAT DEFINES YOU?

Having grown up in a strict Catholic home with legalistic ideals, my vision of marriage was much different from the Lord's, and from my husband's. As a result of life not turning out as I had envisioned, I arrived at a juncture where I felt stuck in a bad place. Between unfounded fears, wanting to control things, and feeling as though I were losing control, I was a mess. I didn't understand Che, and I couldn't seem to help him understand, no matter how many pie charts I went through in trying to break things down for him.

Through our marriage trial, I want to make it clear that we never even entertained the word *divorce,* just the occasional "How about a little truck in his way, Lord."

At one point, I was so depressed, confused, and fearful; voices were coming at me from all sides: Che's, God's, and the devil's. In the confusion, I just didn't know what to do or what direction to take.

"I need *help*, honey," I confessed, hoping he would understand my desperation and the torment I was going through.

"You need to get away for an extra long, really long quiet time, like take three days."

"That's not what I need. I'm really confused, deeply fearful; I don't know what is going on." It was like talking to a wall at times; I couldn't reach him.

By and by, I went for professional counseling, and it really helped. The main thing the counselor conveyed was, "You are not crazy."

Phew, what a relief!

Then I prayed, "Lord, You have to help me; let me see how things are supposed to look here."

For so long I had allowed experiences, circumstances, and the opinions of others to define me, but the Lord said, "Stop."

RELEASE CONTROL

While I am grateful for my Catholic upbringing and what it taught me about sin and obedience, everything in the tradition I grew up in seemed to focus on sin rather than love. It was a list of things we had to do to be loved or to guarantee Heaven, and those things defined who we were.

The 40-day "preparation" period for the observance of Christ's passion and Easter, which is supposed to be an annual opportunity to trace the history of redemption, required us to give up something of significance. Parents were likely to lay down movies or eating out, so it wasn't a popular time for us children. Much superstition and many weird rules, stemming from practices developed by the medieval church, surrounded the observance as well, such as the belief that it was bad luck to wash your face after the Ash Fast. During this time, we would have our foreheads marked with ash. Older kids would tease me that the ashes belonged to dead people. Scary stuff sometimes.

I was five years old; I didn't have much to give up. Candy and gum, a teddy bear, perhaps a pacifier. One day I decided I'd fast candy for a season; however, well before the 40-day mark, I had a lick, well, OK, I sucked on the candy, but I didn't chew. Sometime within that period I also "accidentally" chomped down on the consecrated bread, known as the host, which represented Jesus' body. It got stuck in my molars; I'm not kidding! Chewing it was a mortal sin, and, oh my gosh, I thought, *I'm going to hell.* I could almost imagine it.

> *I thought, I'm going to hell.*

"What are you in for?"

"Sucking on a candy and chewing the Eucharist host."

What's wrong with that picture? Legalism, and it binds us. It sounds humorous, but it is serious stuff because this spirit of religiosity was the core of my fear-based life, which I took into my marriage. The outflow of that religious spirit was a propensity to control things. I was so afraid of making a mistake, so fearful of hell. Talk about bound up! I needed a serious Holy Spirit love makeover, and quick, before the joy went out of my kids as well.

Detox! Get Vision

It took awhile to detox; the cleansing can be a process. As a mother, well, let's just say by ages two or three, each of my children had the Lord's Prayer memorized—a modified version: "Our Father, my mother is sooooo controlling...."

It's true. I wanted them to grow up to be holy according to my picture of holy, and I presented holiness to them in these terms: "No!" "Don't do this; don't do that." I also wanted to look like the perfect mother with good kids.

"You have it all upside down," said the Lord as He started to convict me as well as supply me with a parenting plan. "Number one, enjoy your children."

It is more important to love them than it is to judge them, as it is with all people. At the end of the day, the thing that counts the most when you lay your head on the pillow is how you answer, "How well did I love today? How well did I love my husband, my children, the people around me?"

> *At the end of the day, the thing that counts the most when you lay your head on the pillow is how you answer this question: "How well did I love today?"*

This rang true to my heart because as a little girl, I did want to be a nun, not only to communicate with God but also to be like Mother Teresa, working with children. Nuns just in from missionary work in Africa would visit my classroom in third grade and tell us amazing stories, and I'd think, *I want to do that!*

The next part of God's plan was for me to have a vision and mission statement for parenting, as well as for my marriage and personal life. What core values do you wish to impart? Who are you, and what do you want in life? What are your priorities? How will you get there?

I had my children one after the other, with the first one born a week after our first wedding anniversary; it was the Catholic way! Only twenty-three when I brought little Gabriel home screaming in my arms, I thought, *I don't know what I'm doing; I'm too young; I don't know how to mother.*

"Vision," said God, "You need vision."

Paradigm Shifts

Vision (not to mention motherhood!) changed my paradigm. Wow, I was holding a baby, my firstborn, and this was a child who could potentially change the world and affect lives. Suddenly I could prophetically see into his future and parent from there!

Integrity is core in our house, and a mission I held fast to. My daughter Joy remembers to this day an instance when a drive-through teller gave me an extra 25 cents by mistake, and I went out of my way to get it back to him. I didn't even think Joy noticed as busy as she was slurping on an ice cream cone.

Jamba Juice was opening a new store close by and giving away freebies at their grand opening. I took my daughters with me for some girlie time, and after a forty-five minute wait in line for free juice, finally got back to the car for the drive home.

Just as I turned my head to back the car out, I noticed that Joy didn't have her juice with her.

"What happened to your drink?"

She'd given it to a homeless person way in the back of the line. What a seed she planted, and I'm convinced it was because she'd observed the seed I'd planted at the bank in returning the money to the teller, who could have been held responsible for the overpayment.

Our mission now as parents is to capitalize on teachable moments, moments in love, rather than on the do's or don'ts.

Communication is also important to our marriage and our family. Every Monday is honey time together and family time around the table, where each child shares something encouraging. To this day, we stick to the plan, and when my grown children visit, we still share at the table.

We have a vision as well for our unseen grandchildren and pray often for them. "Lord, we don't know them or see them; they are yet unformed, but as a beautiful painting, You know them, and You have them in Your hands. Please let them know You from an early age; let them follow You all the days of their lives, and choose their spouses, Lord."

I challenge you to ask the Holy Spirit to help you with mission and value statements for your marriage, relationships, ministry, workplace, and anything you're involved with. It will make a difference because you will be able to look straight ahead, directly before you, and walk on level paths and firm ways without swerving to the left or right, tripping up, or stumbling (see Prov. 4:25-27).

THE MEANING OF SIGNIFICANCE

I have learned that when I choose to focus my vision on Jesus and look into His dove-like eyes, I can trust Him with all of my heart to download to me the right plan for life, for marriage, for family, for ministry. Do you know that unlike other birds, when a dove turns its head, its eyes lock in focus. His gaze is on you! When I gaze back, I stay on course, and He is able to perfect my faith to do whatever He needs to do, and He is faithful to complete the good work.

We have personal choices. I could have chosen to remain bonded to the spirits of fear, control, religious spirits, rejection, and legalism, but I made a choice for new wine in a new skin. It did take extra work on God's part, on all of our parts, to bring me to that place of truly knowing who I was and why I was on this earth.

*It is not how much we do,
but how much love we put into it.*

My heroine, tiny and humble Mother Teresa, said that it is the love we put into our actions that matters, not the magnitude of our actions. It is not how much we do, but how much love we put into it.

Joy's Jamba Juice to the homeless man, priceless.

What we do today affects generations for better or for worse. Ultimately the little things we do with much love make the difference, and love comes about by fixing our gaze on Jesus, and what He would do, not what religiosity tells us. I'm happy to tell you, I'm still married to the handsome Asian thirty years later and still insanely in love.

CHRIST'S VISION

Jesus being the very nature of God did not consider equality with God something to be grasped (see Phil. 2:6 NIV).

He had a focused vision.

But made Himself nothing, taking the very nature of a servant, being made in human likeness. And being found in appearance as a man, He humbled Himself and became obedient to death—even death on a cross! (Philippians 2:7-8 NIV).

He lifts your chin, gazes into your eyes, and says, "I have a vision for you, and I pushed through to the Cross for you because I knew what was on the other side."

That vision includes that He who began a good work in you will be faithful to complete it (see Phil. 1:6). That vision includes His focus on you and the plans He has for you, plans for good and not for evil (see Jer. 29:11). That vision is the Father saying to you, "You are My beautiful one, My masterpiece that I display before the universe, and no demon in hell, no past, no present, no height, no depth, no legalism, no mistakes—nothing will be able to separate you from My love!" (See Romans 8:38-39.)

How do I know?

Jesus say so!

PRAYER

Father, I thank You that You give us the choice every moment to fix our eyes on You through the vision of Heaven—Heaven's understanding and its economy—not the vision from below. I thank You that You have called us to be eaglets and eagles with a lioness spirit within to be warriors and protectors of all that is good and right and noble. Thank You for the good work that You have begun in each reader. You are so faithful, having predestined each one of us, and prepared good works for us to accomplish. Holy Spirit, come, and thank You for this divine interruption in our lives that brought us to this place of learning and confidence in Your transformational presence. You are changing us to be like You, to think like You. And so, Father, I thank You and bless Your holy name, in Jesus' name. Amen.

Chapter 8

THE DREAM LIVES ON

by Nina Myers

"Close your eyes," said the woman at a retreat I'd attended, "and picture yourself sitting at home where you normally pray and do devotions."

So I did, imagining myself curled up in my favorite chair in the family room.

"Now, see Jesus enter the room," she said. "What does He say to you?"

The moment I "saw" the Lord, I told Him, "Max is not here."

Wow, why did I say that…as if I did not deem myself worthy of the Lord's attention? As if He would come only to talk to my husband and not me?

Everything seemed to be going OK. My relationship with my husband was amazing. He was being used mightily of God. We were pastoring a great church. I was working as a registered nurse and loved it, and our children were doing well. Granted, I had sort of "forgotten" myself in the midst of trying to keep all the balls in the air...my dreams to birth something bigger than me, to own something...to...to...But then, I'd never really expressed those things to Max or to the Lord.

> *Seeking to understand why I reacted to the Lord as I did was the beginning of a journey through a tunnel of discovery.*

Seeking to understand why I reacted to the Lord as I did was the beginning of a journey through a tunnel of discovery. I'd like to share with you my journey. Many of us find it easy enough to agree in our minds that God truly cares about our lives, about our hopes and dreams, but sometimes the heart finds it difficult to accept. We can get stuck in that dark vacuum, running or shying away from our dreams and the very divine plans of God.

Do You Believe?

Let me ask you, "Do you believe that the Word of the Lord is true?" It is vital that you answer "yes," because His Word is the foundation upon which all of our dreams and hopes are manifested. Over the years we have built or remodeled several homes, I understand the importance of the foundation. We are going to build upon the foundation that the Word of the Lord is true.

We had not been in the new church very long when someone shared that he felt Jeremiah 29:11 was a word of the Lord for me. *"For*

I know the plans that I have for you,' declares the Lord, 'plans for welfare and not for calamity to give you a future and a hope'" (NASB).

I appreciated the sentiment, but my heart did not buy it. The move from Wisconsin to Hutchinson, Minnesota, had been a difficult one for our family. We had been happy pastoring where we were and would have loved to stay there but were not retained, due to a congregation vote. That was a staggering emotional blow since the church was doing so well. I was a little bitter, but what I did not realize at the time was how that translated into a subtle but eventual emotional pulling away from my husband and, I think, also from God. Certainly it birthed some inner resentment: *If we had not been voted out...had you...if only....*

Do You See What God Sees?

The disappointment and upheaval of having to move—the entire journey was a tunnel our family had to walk through. *If God has a plan,* I thought, *I sure wish He would share it with me!*

It just didn't look the way I thought it would.

One night before making the decision to accept the offer of the new church, Max said, "I think God is saying that if we will go to Hutchinson, He will give us the city."

"What if we don't want that city," I pouted. I just couldn't see the fulfillment of our dreams in that place.

Moving up from the foundation of the Word of God to the first floor involves believing the truth that God created you for a purpose and that He has a plan for you. It is buying the plan, seeing beyond your present reality, and knowing that He has your best interest at heart and wants only to give you good gifts. However, often we wish for something else, the grass on the other side of the fence, and as a result we are discontent. "I wish I had her life." "I wish I had her freedom." "I wish my husband was like that." "I want to be over there." "If I only had her job." The "shoulds" can get you too: "I should have spent more time with the kids." "I should be prettier, thinner." "I should pray more." By the time we get done with our self-talk, it is like, "Gosh, I don't know what to do anymore—I can't do anything!" I caution against dissatisfaction and regret because every season is special and meant to be different. Each season is a stepping stone toward the fulfillment of God-planted dreams, as are our mistakes, which ultimately should propel us forward in wisdom, not hold us back.

> *Each season is a stepping stone toward the fulfillment of God-planted dreams.*

TUNNEL TIME

The rubber meets the road on the second floor. That is living out the plan, which can be a journey where you do not always see the proverbial light at the end of the tunnel. In my case, it took awhile to see it. Tunnel traffic may look like any one or a combination of these things in your life:

- You cannot see beyond your present circumstance.

- You may seem to have it all together, but feel lost.

- Like Sarah, you feel past the point of birthing something.

- You have a dream, a desire, a longing; it is there, but you are not sure what to do with it.

- Something inside of you says, "Someday I would love to...." or "I want more, but I'm not even sure what 'more' looks like...."

- You've had a prophetic word, and it is too big, too far out there—you can't see it happening.

- You are impatient, and you want it now. Like yesterday already!

- You don't feel qualified, or able, or capable, and through negative self-talk, which is what many women struggle with, you become your own worst enemy.

- You may feel inferior, or of no value or significance to God to be used for any sort of greatness.

- Or, *nothing* seems to be going right.

As a result, if we are not careful, we can become frustrated and resentful toward God, toward our circumstances, and/or toward others. These are places you do not want to visit.

PLANS TO PROSPER YOU

Whenever Max and I travel, we try to avoid chain restaurants and fast food outlets, instead we seek out unique, quaint places to eat. One day while sitting in a cafe overlooking the main street of a town we were visiting, I said, "Hutchinson needs something like this, a nice coffee/espresso place."

It had always been a dream of mine to open a restaurant. I had talked about it for years but never followed through. Hutchinson, a community of 15,000 people with no coffee shop, was ripe.

"Well," said Max, "are you going to do this, or not?" In other words, there was a void; it was time to put wheels on the dream. Enough talk. Do it already!

Say what? I'd never even had a latte! It was scary, and I could think of every excuse why I couldn't do it. For one, I was a nurse, not a business whiz.

"Um, OK," I said, not knowing how I'd even get it off the ground. Still a little unsure and not wanting to dive in financially or commit to anything major right way, I took a safe baby step and asked my son, Jeff, who worked in real estate, to register the business "Coffee Company" with the state.

Max and I in the meantime departed for Israel with a tour group from the church. While we were away, Jeff emailed me.

"I heard that someone is looking to open a new coffee shop in town—searching out commercial property."

Uh oh. Time to get serious now, to commit.

"Run an ad in the newspaper, OK? Have it say, "Coffee Company Is Coming.""

"But, Mom, you don't even have a location. What do I put in for an address?"

"Never mind that, just please run the ad," I said. I knew that if I did not commit right then, I'd either lose the advantage of being the first coffee house in the city, or, the dream would lose its sizzle once I got back into my usual routine at home.

Almost the moment we touched down at the airport, Jeff buzzed us and asked us to meet him downtown to view a potential shop location he'd found. This was it! I signed the lease right away.

*Now that I had truly committed to the dream,
the Lord sent me help.*

Now that I had truly committed to the dream, the Lord sent me help, and it was a supernaturally amazing thing to watch how things seamlessly unfolded. As it happened, a couple in our church had a son who owned several coffee shops in a town an hour away. They arranged a meeting, and he connected us to the world of espresso. My husband, a natural handyman, did the remodeling, and my son's business background proved an ongoing invaluable asset.

I was right, coffee was just what Hutchinson needed and soon proved a popular place with the locals. Moreover, people loved the tangible atmosphere: "It feels different…this can't be Hutchinson." Indeed, I'd hoped for that wow factor by offering the best experience ever, and if it wasn't, we'd make it right for the customer.

One day the Lord showed me how this store had truly served to change people. I had hired a young and struggling single mother although everything in the natural at the initial interview screamed, "No, don't take her on!" She already held two other jobs, her availability was limited, and she was trying to get her life on track, with limited success. She refused to wear her name badge, and if she did wear one, it belonged to someone else. By and by, the godly atmosphere changed her, and one morning she arrived wearing five badges, all bearing her real name. It was overwhelming and touched me deeply. She became very dear to me over the years.

With the resounding success of store one, glory to God, He continued to s-t-r-e-t-c-h me. One year after our opening, Max said, "Come on, I want to show you something," and took me to see an old gas station up for rent.

"Why don't you consider this as a second shop? It's a mile away, and close to the mall."

Two stores! I was busy enough. Max didn't let up, however, and persistently, gently prodded.

The second Coffee Company opened almost one year to the day of our first location and proved even more popular, profitable, and life changing. It still amazes me how supernaturally successful it was.

Fourteen years after we moved to Hutchinson, Max said, "God gave us the city, but it wasn't through the church as I had thought. It was your coffee shop."

Anything is possible when you allow God to guide you through the tunnel. He helps you through it peacefully with the confidence that He who designed you will guide you throughout the process.

I do believe in God's timing. It was the right season for me to open those shops and that season opened up my present one.

Your dream is not hopeless. If God has called you to it, it is not impossible because it is purposed by the hand of God Himself. He who deems you beautiful, capable, without spot or blemish. His divine design. Priceless.

Abigail's Tunnel

Abigail, whose name means "the joy of her father" was an intelligent and beautiful woman, but she was married to the harsh, evil, and very rich Nabal (whose name means "the fool") of the house of Caleb. He was a disgrace to his family, to the Calebites; far from inheriting his ancestor's virtues, he was always surly, snappish, greedy. His wealth was very great but not his wisdom or grace. (See First Samuel 25.)[1]

She was the opposite, a woman of great beauty of the heart and understanding. Her demeanor itself was such a testimony. Her father had given Abigail to be married to a man, more interested in his wealth than in his daughter's happiness. This likely was her tunnel. She had no idea what God would do through her or for her, or even if He would. She was in her present circumstance and could not see the future plan God had for her.

At David's dispatch, his mighty men humbly requested of Nabal food and supplies for their camp; Nabal turned them down, waving them off even though his own shepherds had received from David and his men much kindness and even protection from the plundering and roving Philistines. Even though he was anointed king and could have specifically ordered Nabal to hand over supplies, or taken them by force, David did not demand. He was, no doubt, expecting a return of favors—that his men would return well-laden with provisions.

Word of her husband's denial of the request got to Abigail by way of one of the young men who knew David well. He had reason to think David would highly resent the affront, and may even have had information of David's orders to his men to march that way. This man alerted Abigail to the fact that they would not be able to resist the force David would bring down upon them; they would not have time to send for Saul's protection. Something needed to be done to pacify King David.

Unbeknown to her husband, Abigail made haste and took the best of her house: loaves, wine, ready-dressed sheep, parched corn, clusters of raisins, and fig cakes; she loaded them on the donkeys, then climbed on one herself, and brought them to David to atone for her husband's denial of their request.

She knew her makeup and well-stewarded her gifting.

She made haste. She did not talk herself out of it. She knew her makeup and well-stewarded her gifting. Her engaging wisdom and virtue greatly influenced history. She convinced David not to shed innocent blood or do something he would later regret. Who knows how things would have looked—had she not? Someone once said, "You have to dream so big and have such a big plan that God would be embarrassed not to do something."

We do know that as a result of journeying through the tunnel God's way, lives are saved, Nabal dies, and Abigail marries King David of Israel—the greatest king to ever rule the Holy Land, a warrior, poet, and man after God's heart.

IT IS A NEW DAY FOR WOMEN

You have a role of significance in the Kingdom of God, because you were born into that role. You are the joy of the Father. For too long, religiosity and theology have prevented women from moving forward, even into leadership roles, but that is changing. It is a new hour and a new day. It is time to shake off the old thinking.

You step here or there, and people say, "Oh, but that's not right." It is so not true, not true. Saddle up; load the donkeys; your contribution can change history. We bear the image of Jesus Christ; His nature and His character is in each one of us, male and female.

My tunnel journey brought me a greater understanding of the plans and purposes of God in my life as a Christian, as a wife, as a mother, as a marketplace leader, as a ministry leader, as a friend, and as a woman. It has rendered me a deeper relationship with my husband, a greater appreciation of how God uses my design for maximum impact, and joyful acceptance of His design for me and my life.

Indeed, when I "see" Jesus today, it is not, "Max isn't here," but, "Here am I, Lord," and I dream on.

Nina's Tunnel Tips

- Don't be afraid to verbalize your dreams. Speak them. Do not hold them in. Cry out to God; tell Him what you want deep inside. Tell Him, "I don't want to go to my grave having never done/seen/experienced...."

- Avoid talking yourself into defeat. Don't let your imagination or thoughts conjure false scenarios by way of the "shoulds," and the "should haves."

- Ask the Lord to search your heart for resentment and bitterness; forgive, repent, and receive His forgiveness.

- Your dreams, passions, and destiny are unique to you. Your giftings and talents are also unique, and God wants to use them to take you to the next place.

- Let your imagination go wild. Dream and realize that what is inside you is not only a good idea, but more than possible because it is God-inspired.

Prayer

Father, I want to see these beautiful women set free to dream, to step into destiny. Please release them to dream, to know that You can use them abundantly more than they can ever imagine. Help them to see what You really have for them, to help them go beyond where they are at. Bless their dreams and visions. Thank You for putting them here, reading this today for this time. Thank You for the desire You have deposited within them—the ideas, the creativity. You have given each one something supernatural to change the world, and You have given them spheres of influence. Please continue to grant them favor, prosperity at home, in ministry, and in the marketplace, such that everyone who comes within their spheres will notice remarkable atmospheric change. Reveal the value of their gifts and talents, of their strengths and weaknesses. Please Father, in Jesus' name, I ask You to open their eyes to their responsibility to carry Your heart. Open doors, create divine connections, help them to move when You move, and to rest in Your strength. Amen!

ENDNOTE

1. *Matthew Henry's Commentary on the Whole Bible* (Peabody, MA: Hendrickson Publishers, 2008); 1 Samuel 25.

Part III

BEAUTIFUL
Dreamer
AWAKE UNTO ME

See! The winter is past; the rains are over and gone.
Flowers appear on the earth; the season of singing has come,
the cooing of doves is heard in our land.
The fig tree forms its early fruit; the blossoming vines
spread their fragrance. Arise, come, my darling;
my beautiful one, come with me
(Song of Solomon 2:11-13 NIV).

Our Father in Heaven is not a give-a-little God but Creator God who will stop the sun to help us complete the work He has given us, and who will send a heavenly host to help us fight every breakthrough battle in our lives. Nothing you have need of within the Lord's plans for you is too large to ask. Transition is not hard when you awaken Heaven. As you ride the waves of change, liberate and refresh yourself by asking for all the bliss you need in abundance: justice, healing, protection, truth, beauty of the heart, righteousness, heavenly gifts, second chances, salvation, financial provision. It all belongs to you because you belong to God! As you read the following chapters by Beni, Anne, Winnie, DeAnne, and Heidi, you will learn to breathe again and experience the release and profound peace of God on your journey.

Chapter 9

WAKEY WAKEY!

by *Beni Johnson*

Suddenly a great company of the heavenly host
appeared with the angel, praising God and saying,
"Glory to God in the highest,
*and on earth **peace to men on whom His favor rests***"
(Luke 2:13-14 NIV).

*W*e are on a verge of another awakening. I have seen it in my life, in our family, and in a great increase of miracles, signs, wonders, and breakthrough in our ministry.

When the devastating December 26, 2004, Indian Ocean earthquake hit off the west coast of Sumatra, Indonesia, causing a huge tsunami, I felt in my spirit the *shifting* of the earth's physical plates. I spoke to a prophet I'd met and asked him about it. "Do you think the plates shifted, and do you believe that this is the beginning of something spiritual about to happen?"

"Yes," he said, "because usually a spiritual event follows a physical one."

I am convinced that the Indonesia disaster, hear my heart, as devastating as it was in the natural, was the beginning of something grand in the supernatural things of God. By no means does God cause disaster, but He can take anything bad, turn it around, and use it for His purposes. Accordingly, I feel we are on the verge of a huge spiritual shift and breakthrough. I can feel it; we are deep inside Isaiah 60. How exciting to be in the moment of *"Arise, shine, for your light has come, and the glory of the Lord rises upon you. See, darkness covers the earth and thick darkness is over the peoples, but the Lord rises upon you and His glory appears over you"* (Isa. 60:1-2 NIV).

It Is Time to Focus

My husband, Bill, and I have held onto the promises of Isaiah 60 for thirty years. We sense that this is that time! It is time to say, "This is who I am," and focus, for we are potentially in a time of transition in labor, which happens right before a baby is born.

When my youngest daughter, Leah, was pregnant, she with her husband decided the baby's delivery would be *au naturel,* as I had done with all three of my children in the 1970s, when natural childbirth was the *in* thing, and meds were totally out. "Can you like, be my coach, Mom?"

I sensed her husband was relieved by the prospective role change, "Oh, I'll be *in* there…you know, cheering her on, handing her the washcloths, the ice chips…."

Yeah right, the not-so-gooey, easy stuff. Of course I would help them, I was honored to be asked, and Leah and her husband wanted the support of someone who'd been there before….

Wow! I forgot how much labor it is to have a baby. "The coaching," I told Bill just after Judah was born, "was the hardest work I've done since I had our kids!" And I meant it.

If you have had natural childbirth or have midwived, you especially understand the three distinct stages of the process of labor: latent, active, and transition, each stage increasing in intensity. In the active stage, contractions are longer and stronger, with more back pain and a need to concentrate on the labor process. The coach is close by to provide comfort, encouragement, and help with relaxing through breathing exercises.[1]

When the mother enters into the transition phase, the contractions intensify as the baby applies pressure to her bottom area. Mom has to concentrate on not pushing against the pressure until given the OK by the medical team.[2] This stage just before the actual birth, especially, can be distressing. It is the emotional part of labor where you just don't want to do it anymore, and if your husband touches you, you're in trouble, buddy! You can get confused and disoriented, and want to give up and go home. If you could keep the baby inside of you somehow, you would, and you just don't think you can endure it for another minute. Often the most important role of a birth coach or support person is to talk the mom through this panicky, sometimes distressing period, and give her the encouragement and focus she needs to finish the job, to do what she needs to do for a healthy delivery. It is a time when the coach can see what she perhaps cannot.

There were times, especially during the transition phase, that Leah and I were head-to-head. "Honey, you are going to do this."

"I don't think I can."

"Yes, yes, you can—you *are* going to do this. You will do this."

Just as I got her back on focus midway through a contraction, a friend popped into the room for a visit. She wasn't paying attention to what was happening with Leah and was chatting with others in the room. I thought, *What is she doing? Can't she see we're trying to have a baby here?*

"Shhh—," I said, and motioned toward Leah, hoping that the interruption had not caused a shift of focus onto the pain.

> *What is she doing?*
> *Can't she see we're trying to have a baby here?*

After the delivery and once she'd settled in, I asked my daughter, "Did her visit bother you, cause you to lose focus? I mean, she wasn't even paying attention."

"Mom, I was so tuned in to your voice, on what you were telling me to do, and on your eyes, that I didn't even notice."

EMBRACE GOD, EMBRACE TRANSITION

Later, I thought, *Oh my gosh, that is what we need to do with Jesus.* We need to *embrace* what's happening and *position ourselves* with our *eyes on Jesus, seeing* and *hearing* what He is saying to us, how He is directing and leading us, no matter how intense the circumstances.

I love a good storm—rain, lightning, and thunder—but some people dive for cover at the first sharp, loud crack or long, low rumble. Many believers react in the same way to dramatic shifts of change—good or bad—in their personal lives, their families, businesses, churches, the government, and the nations. Like it or not, however, and as painful as it may be, change is happening, and, I'm convinced, more so in the coming days. Perfect storms are on the horizon, so my encouragement to you is to embrace this transition phase even if painful, for in embracing it, we learn what God is revealing in these exciting days. The labor phase doesn't stop until after the delivery of all that God has promised you in a situation.

By the way, the devil does not want you to know who you are, or how much God loves you. Nor does he want you to soak in the presence of God or discover the greatest secret of intimacy—because once you engage so personally with God, you become a powerful weapon. No one can stop you. Once you see the burning eyes of Jesus burning for you, nothing will stop you.

A whole breed of saints who have been on their faces before God are rising up with incredible strategy, direction, and hope. "Laid down lovers," as Heidi Baker terms these saints, are arising and shining. In His presence, eye-to-eye, is where to be in times of transition and birthing the new; in His presence in the sanctuary is where we discover what is going on. As the previously lamenting, distressed, and complaining psalmist discovered,

> But when I thought how to understand this, it seemed to me a wearisome task, until I went into the sanctuary of God; then I discerned their end....Nevertheless, I am continually with You; You hold my right hand. You guide me with Your counsel, and afterward You will receive me to glory (Psalm 73:16-17;23-24 ESV).[3]

Unless we go into the sanctuary, into the presence of God and keep our eyes focused on Him, we won't know what is going on; we won't have the determination that Luke observed in Luke 9:51 of Jesus who "set His face to go to Jerusalem." To set one's face is to choose, to move, to create a new direction, a new meaning. Christ chose to focus on what

He was set to do, and so must we, and it is that much easier when we know and understand.

The presence of God *is* our secret weapon against the devil; that is where God wants to take us and wants us to stay. Are you in that place?

> *The presence of God is*
> *our secret weapon against the devil.*

If you are going through a tough time right now, if something has shifted in your life and you are awaiting breakthrough, Jesus is saying, "You can; you are going to do this; you will get it done. You will have this baby. Yes, you will."

It's what you need to hear to get through transition. "The baby's head is crowning."

We are living in the most exciting days to be alive ever, ever, ever. Tell yourself that every day if you have to.

Say it out loud, now: I am living in the most exciting time ev-er!

WHAT ARE THESE TIMES?

It is obvious in our nation today that we really need God and must press into Him. For this reason, God is raising up people right now to birth a new movement, an outpouring greater than this earth has ever seen.

In Cardiff, Wales, a young boy, Seth Joshua, decided to skip school to go fishing. While fishing the stream, he heard his father approach, and he hid in the bushes. As his dad walked the trail, Seth heard him cry out to the Father, "God, give me Wales; God give me Wales."

When the youngster returned home, he asked his mother, "Why is father praying that?"

"Son," she replied, "someday you will know, and you will understand."

Seth Joshua grew up, and when he became a young man, he followed his father into ministry. Walking the same trail, he prayed, "God give me Wales; God give me Wales," but added to his prayer, "God, bring me a young man, bring me a young man, not learned—a man from the mines or a simple carpenter—but a young man. Give me Wales; give me Wales."[4]

In the years leading up to 1904, there were many indications from most of Wales that a time of awakening was happening, with crowded churches, new professions of faith, and a new resolve toward righteousness. Seth Joshua was then holding special meetings in a church near Cardigan in Blaenannerch. One day, a young man, twenty-six-year-old Evan Roberts, born near Swansea, the ninth of fourteen children, walked into the meeting, having traveled there to attend Seth's Gospel meetings with other students from a preparatory ministry school in Newcastle Emlyn. Evan was deeply serious about serving God and had been accepted as a candidate for the ministry by the Calvinistic Methodists in 1904, and had just begun his studies thinking he would go to seminary in 1906. Interestingly, he himself had been praying for years for revival and an outpouring of the Holy Spirit. Through a vision he received, Roberts believed that God was going to win 100,000 souls.

As a youngster of twelve years he had worked in a coal mine, and in 1902, he apprenticed to his uncle who was a blacksmith; thus, he had every qualification as an answer to Seth's prayers.

Let's just say Evan got hit by the Holy Spirit big time: he was filled and baptized, receiving an anointing of the Holy Spirit with great power. So deeply affected was he that he requested to leave his studies to return to his home church to share his blessings with his peers. At his first meeting on a Monday night in 1904, the heavens opened; God's presence filled the atmosphere; many were moved by what they heard, prostrated with conviction. Others cried out for mercy, and many, many were filled with the Holy Spirit. Then the multitudes came.

Evan, his friends, and teams of young people spread out, throughout South Wales, sharing their ministry of exhortation, praise, and prayer. Other preachers stepped up their efforts. Newspapers began to report the day-to-day news, and people traveled from far and near to hear the message. Revival then grasped North Wales. Within six months, 100,000 had come to Christ!

News spread around the world about the Welsh Revival causing passionate prayer and igniting revival fires around the globe. Great Britain, Scandinavia, Germany, Austria, Poland, Hungary, the Balkans, Slovakia, and Russia also experienced awakenings. The U.S. felt its aftershock in almost every state. The Church grew.

In California, a man named William Seymour started corresponding with Evan Roberts, and through their contact, a revival broke out in 1906. The Holy Spirit descended on Azusa Street, birthing the modern Pentecostal Movement. Daily meetings were held there for three years, and multitudes flocked to catch the power of the Spirit—and they were not disappointed! You can read detailed accounts in an amazing book entitled, *Azusa Street: They Told Me Their Stories.*[5]

> *Multitudes flocked to catch the power of the Spirit.*

Who knew that the spark, the cries of one father for his nation, would ignite the beginning of the greatest and most effective global evangelistic movement, outreach, and Holy Spirit outpouring the world had until then ever seen or known? And guess what?

William Seymour later prophesied an even *greater outpouring to come*, a hundred years hence, as did another man, Charles Parham on the East coast. They prophesied another world awakening, and if you do the math, we are in that time. How exciting![6] The baby is about to crown! No wonder we are in a time of intensity!

ARE YOU A LILY LIVING IN POVERTY FLATS?

The journey through transition to birthing something new can be especially difficult with a poverty mindset, which keeps us in fear and with a skewed perception of God. I know poverty and grew up in it, in a real town known at the time as Poverty Flats. "Abundance" and "overflowing" were not categories I lived in, and I did not realize that my impoverished mentality clung to me in such a way that when the Lord began to pour out His blessings on me, I could not receive.

The instant God revealed the problem, I made up for lost time. "Father, I am so sorry and receive *all* of Your blessings."

The poverty spirit can seep into the way we speak and rob us of our blessings.

I can't…

God won't…

It's impossible…

It won't happen to me…

It is time to go on a negativity fast! We did that in our church once, and it was the hardest fast ever.

> *Just recognizing*
> *where you've been living*
> *is the beginning of the shift.*

Just recognizing where you've been living is the beginning of the shift. Give the Holy Spirit permission to arrest your mouth and your thinking against negative thoughts and believe that God's grace is sufficient for hard situations. Believe that God is in control, even if you do not understand what in the world He is doing, even if it is not the way you would do it. Put your hand on your heart right now and tell Him, "You are in control; I trust only You, God. I say 'Yes' to all that You are doing, I say 'Yes' to the most exciting time to live. Yes, in Jesus' name."

FEAR NOT

Every time Leah had a contraction during the transitional phase of her labor, we would speak peace over her. Increasingly, the Lord has been speaking to my heart concerning transition, which most of us are experiencing, and saying, "Don't be afraid of sudden fear." The Lord wants you to give Him full control of any panicky situation or circumstance that causes you worry or pain. Indeed, let the *shalom* (peace) of Heaven, the peace that passes all understanding, that of "completeness, wholeness, health, welfare, safety, soundness, tranquility, prosperity, perfection, fullness, rest, harmony, and the absence of agitation or discord"[7] come to you, in Jesus' name.

Step in and cultivate peace. In other words, with eyes on Jesus, declare into the atmosphere that you will no longer be afraid, that the Lord Jesus Christ is in full control. In the midst of all the chaos going on in the world or within our own spheres of influence, we can stand and be people of peace, walking not only into our own destinies with expectation of spiritual, physical, or emotional change, but also into neighborhoods, cities, government offices, schools, hospitals, churches, stadiums, and wherever you go—for whatever the need or circumstance.

WAKE THE ANGELS TO ASSIST YOU

Angels are among us—messenger angels, healing angels, fiery angels—and they are here for many reasons. They have been bored for a long time and are ready to be put to work helping to usher the Kingdom of God into our realm! As we begin to recognize that they are among us, we will begin to see more angelic activity as we pull Heaven to earth into our lives, into the world. Like a medical team at the ready to assist the birth, angels are ready to assist in the birth of breakthrough.[8]

> *Like a medical team at the ready to assist the birth, angels are ready to assist in the birth of breakthrough.*

Before one of our international students moved to Redding, California, from Wales in the UK to attend our supernatural school at Bethel, she had a divine visitation. "Sue,"[9] was awakened in the middle of the night by the weighty presence of God; a visible glory cloud filled her room. The Lord spoke to her. "I want you to go to Moriah Chapel and say, "'Wakey wakey.'"

You want me to do wha-a-t?

Moriah Chapel is where Evan Roberts carried much of the revival! I visited it recently, and today it stands as a monument and memorial place of that great outpouring. Sue could not understand why God would ask such a thing and wrestled with Him.

"I'm sorry, God, but I'm not doing *that!*"

But God said to her again, "I want you to go to Moriah Chapel and say, "'Wakey wakey.'"

At that point, Sue knew that if she did not do it, she would regret it for the rest of her life, so the next day she headed out to the chapel at a time she thought would not be busy with tourists, but she arrived to a crowd. She asked God why it was so busy, and He said, "Because I had to tell you twice!"

So she stood there and did as God had asked her. "Wakey wakey," she declared in a half whisper.

"Is that how bad you want it, how much you desire revival in Wales?" God asked.

She raised her voice considerably: *"Wakey Wakey!"*

Nothing happened for a few moments, so she decided to leave. Just as she turned, however, the ground shook, and she heard a huge yawn. Glancing back, she saw a huge angel: "—the foot was as big as the chapel." *Big* angel! Guess what? She had the courage to speak to this giant divine being. "Who are you?" she asked.

"I am the angel from the 1904 revival, and you just woke me up," he replied.

"Why have you been asleep?"

"Because no one has been calling out for revival anymore."

Sue asked him if he was the angel that would bring the next revival, and he replied "No, a bigger angel is coming—a bigger move is coming."[10]

It is time for us to stir up the angels to help us carry out God's plans for major breakthrough and revival in our homes, cities, and nations. They are ready, and there are plenty of them!

ANGELS WE HAVE HEARD ON HIGH[11]

I don't know about you, but that would really get me excited; having a visitation like that would really shake me up! I like angels and find they love to show up when we talk about them. When they come, they bring the presence of God. In the past few months, especially, I have become more aware of angelic activity in our realm. One of those times was on a prayer trip to Arizona. My assistant one day suggested, "You need to do something about Sedona, Arizona." I told her I would pray about it, and asked God, "What should I do?"

I felt we were supposed to go there and pray to release more of God's Kingdom. So I gathered some female intercessors, and instead of flying, we decided to rent an RV for all six of us in Sacramento, California, and we would head out from there. What a hoot and crazy, wonderful journey it was! With no real agenda or schedule to keep, we stopped often along the way to Sedona to pray if we felt impressed to do so. When we arrived in Bakersfield, California, I turned left and up into the mountain ridge area of beautiful Tehachapi Pass (elevation 3,793 feet), home of the Tehachapi Pass Wind Farm, one of California's largest.

Sweetly Singing O'er the Plains

The windmills were an awesome sight; the wind propelling the turbines reminding me of angels and of God riding on the wind. Something stirred within me to press on quickly. At the top of the pass, the Mojave Desert, miles and miles of it, spread out below us.

On our descent, in the distance, the impression of the presence of angels grew stronger, and I thought I "saw" angelic-like shapes far below, dotting the desert landscape. As we descended and drew nearer, I was sure of it. "There are like angels out there—and lots of 'em! I wonder what they are doing there; we *have* to stop." I was so excited because whenever angels are present, I know that God is up to something big.

On our descent, in the distance, the impression of the presence of angels grew stronger.

We found an exit, took it, and drove into the small town of Mohave, not really knowing what to do or where to go, we just knew that something was going on, and we needed to discover what it was. As we drove around a corner onto Highway 58, I said, "I have a feeling we will be waking up some angels here." No sooner had I said that than we drove past a hotel to our left: the "*Mariah* Country Inn." The connection was immediately evident to us, even though the spelling and pronunciation was a little different. Recall the wakey wakey angel in the Moriah Chapel in Wales?

Celebrate: Gloria in Exelsis Deo!

Scr-e-e-e-ch! We pulled a U-turn, just knowing we were to stop and wake up the angels. I wish I could convey the energy and quickness of how God worked that day. We all jumped out of the RV; I blew the shofar and rang the bell,[12] and everyone yelled, *"Wakey Wakey!"* We all piled back into the vehicle laughing; it was hilarious and a celebration. The presence of God was so strong, and everything had happened so quickly; we were spinning from the adventure. Heaven had collided with earth, and we were there. Woo hoo!

I recall another time while were having a conference at Bethel, with Randy Clark as a guest speaker. Randy had lost his Bible somewhere at the church, but we could not find it anywhere. One of our gals who enjoys God's angels and gets fairly whacked when they are around because God's presence is so thick, announced to a friend of mine who had also been searching for the Bible with us, that she saw an angel, and that in fact, it was standing beside her.

"Well, why don't you ask the angel where Randy's Bible is?" he said.

She did exactly that. Suddenly she turned, walked toward our administration building straight into Bill's office, got down on the floor, reached between the couch and the coffee table, and pulled out Randy's Bible.

Angels are here, and they are among us.

Angels are here, and they are among us. Be ready to employ them when you are supposed to. We do not worship angels, nor do we order them around, but we should not be ignoring them either. They are here to carry out God's Kingdom. We have noticed that they also like having fun and being among us. They have been sent to assist us, and we need all the help we can get. I, for one, am ready and willing, and God is releasing more. So get ready. They will come at times when you least expect them.

Later in telling the story about our angel RV ride at my church, one of our members reminded me, "Well, you know, John the Baptist was in the desert preparing the way for the Lord. Perhaps these angels are preparing the way for the Lord too." Angels always seem to usher in moves of God. Consider Gabriel coming to Mary and telling her that she would conceive, or the angels announcing Christ's birth.

I was in Norway awhile ago speaking at a prayer center, and as I recounted the wakey wakey stories, a woman came up to me and said, "Ah, now I know what happened, what I saw. Right outside the center here, one day, I saw a giant sit up out of the ground. Now I understand it. It had to have been an angel."[13]

Oh my goodness, how our wakey wakey stories have spread; it has to be so significant that we know to awaken the angels, that we know of their availability, that they are waking up as God activates the Body of Christ to be signs and wonders and revivalists in the land, changing atmospheres, and letting the world know that we know who we are, and to prepare them for the shock and awe of God's love.

JOY TO THE WORLD

It is not about calling down consuming fire as Elijah did, but of the whole other "life" way of the New Covenant way that Jesus brought. In the Old Covenant, if you touched a leper, you were unclean. In the New, when Jesus touched the leper, the leper became clean. It is an entirely new paradigm. Jesus wants us to bring the right Spirit with us into our lives and into the world, not a divided, judgmental, accusatory one, but a unified, compassionate, and passionate One, presenting a joyful, loving Savior. If we want a great awakening, we have to love and exuberantly exude joy to the world.

Have you entered the joy of the Lord? Jesus did and endured the Cross because of the joy set before Him. We are living in exciting, intense times of grand adventure. Blow the shofars, ring your bells, awaken the angels, set your face toward your promised land, and enter into the joy of the Lord as the baby crowns.

ENDNOTES

1. Information adapted from Expectant Mother's Guide to Philadelphia: Stages of Labor: What to Expect During Childbirth; Stage 1: (Contractions and Dilating). See http://www.expectantmothersguide.com/library/philadelphia/EPHlabor.htm; accessed January 24, 2010.

2. Ibid.

3. Please do read the entire psalm for a fuller understanding.

4. Paraphrased.

5. J. Edward Morris, Cindy McCowan, *Azusa Street: They Told Me Their Stories* (Mustang, OK: Dare2Dream, 2006).

6. Some details have been added or verified to Beni's paraphrased accounts of the Welsh Revival with information gleaned from the following Web sites: The Revival Library article: "The Sixth Worldwide Awakening of 1904—The Welsh Revival," *http://www.revival-library.org/catalogues/1904ff/index1904.html;* accessed January 24, 2010. Banner of Truth article: "The 1904 Revival in Wales," *http://www.banneroftruth.org/pages/articles/article_detail.php?713;* accessed January 24, 2010.

7. "Shalom"; see Strong's Concordance 7965.

8. Introduction to this section from an online video of Beni's account of this story to another group.

9. Name changed.

10. Many people in Wales have since seen that angel since our student awoke him.

11. This and the following two subheadings are lyrics from the carol, "Angels We Have Heard on High" translated from French to English by James Chadwick, 1862. Interestingly, this hymn was originally a traditional French carol entitled, "Les Anges dans nos Campagnes," which translated means, "Angels in our Midst."

12. Intercession is often accomplished in the same way that Jesus accomplished it when He walked the earth: through the Word, worship, prayer, and prophetic acts. Sometimes the latter are very powerful, especially when used to bring spiritual release. We often use our instruments for their sounds' prophetic significance, such as the sound of a bell for the sound of Kingdom provision, or bells of grace; or the shofar for a birthing or heralding of something new; or drums as a battle cry, and so on.

13. Paraphrased.

Chapter 10

CATCHING WAVES OF CHANGE

by *Anne Stock*

Forty years ago almost a half million bell-bottomed, tie-dyed, long-haired, glassy-eyed young people descended upon a 600-acre dairy farm near Woodstock, New York. Billed as a "peaceful" anti-establishment, anti-war protest, thirty-two music acts performed during this weekend-long, "aquarian (Age of Aquarius) exposition" from August 15-18, 1969, to "complain," about the Vietnam war, about leaders, about the older generation. On day three, psychedelic rock group Country Joe and the Fish, led the crowd in a defiant remake of its famous F-I-S-H cheer: "Give me an F, give me a U, give me a—." This was likely the loudest and longest sound of cursing, dishonor, and complaint ever heard, the collective sound of a desperate, disillusioned generation telling off the industrial-military complex, their parents, and "the establishment."[1]

The Woodstock Festival was in some ways the high point of the countercultural revolution that marked a turning point in our culture. The disgruntled youth of that generation were sucked into a swirl of discontent: in a manner similar to the Israelites who did not want to go to war, distrusted their leaders, and felt as grasshoppers among giants.

A Big Wave Is Coming

We find ourselves again in a time of historical opportunity. Heaven responds when a generation seeks. This time, there are millions of whole-hearted worshipers who can seize the moment to define the sound of what is coming.

We can detonate a new sound!

A sound of love, unity, humility, and honor!

Lately, we keep hearing that something very big and very good is on the horizon. Bill Johnson calls it "the revival that never ends." Our friend, prophet Kim Clement declares that this coming move of God will be an "accumulation of every move of the Spirit of the past 2,000 years. God will wrap up in one package and pour it out on one generation." A generation comprises all those living at one time. So, if you are alive and breathing, you qualify to have this "accumulated package" poured out on you. The waves of revival are rolling in!

We want to catch these waves of unprecedented opportunity. Our family loves water. We all enjoy body surfing, especially with boogie boards. To catch the best waves, you need to watch for what is coming and move to the best places. Experience is a great teacher.

How can we prepare ourselves for the waves of revival? I've been making observations and identifying patterns that can help us position ourselves for this new thing. The two major turning points in my own personal history were the Jesus Wave of 1972, and the Renewal Wave of 1994.

THE JESUS WAVE: 1972

My husband and I met Jesus in 1972, caught in a wave of miracles and evangelism that swept the earth, often referred to as the Jesus Movement. We were birthed into revival and have revival in our spiritual DNA. Evangelized by the manifest presence of God's glory in simple worship gatherings, we heard testimonies and saw inexplicable miracles with our own eyes. Our world and our lives were altered in this huge flood of grace. What positioned us to catch that big wave? I have identified four factors.

Diligence. We were misguided but diligent in our search for answers. We read books and attended lectures by gurus and psychedelic leaders. We tried all kinds of Eastern religions, philosophies, disciplines, and mystical practices. Even standing on our heads and our extreme brown rice diet was an expression of our efforts to find the Truth, to find God.

Desperation. Along with so many in our generation, we couldn't find satisfaction in the prevailing culture around us. I've observed that in crucial seasons of time, preceding personal or corporate revival, there seems to be what I term "pre-revival misery," characterized by *dis-* words. People feel disillusioned, discouraged, disheartened, dissatisfied, discontented, disappointed, and more. We couldn't find peace in new age religions, nature, health foods, or even each other. My desperation mounted when someone poisoned my dog. Molly had been a close comfort to me through my college years, and the loss catapulted me into thinking about life after death. It was a setup. I don't believe God caused Molly's death, but He used it. Our losses make us desperate enough to search for Truth and open enough to let Truth come inside.

A Hurdle. John Wimber said, "God will offend our minds to reveal our hearts." There is often something in our worldview that keeps us from true spiritual progress. The Gospel of Jesus Christ seemed too simple to me. One man died on the Cross for all people of all time? I felt that the answer must be more complicated, more difficult to attain, surely requiring hard work and intense effort.

Humble Response. I was willing to concede that perhaps I didn't have the big picture. I made the best offer I could, telling the Lord that I would immerse myself in "everything Jesus" for six months and asked Him to show me He was real. God kindly calculated my stupidity into the whole equation of His grace, and my life changed forever. To catch this wave of new life in Christ, I had to humble myself.

The Renewal Wave: 1994

Another wave of God's move twenty-two years later revealed a similar pattern.

Diligence and faithfulness? Yes, I qualified. As a Christian by then for over two decades and a pastor's wife for almost as long, I'd been faithful in my walk: reading my Bible from cover-to-cover once a year, tithing, fasting, and praying, and sacrificially giving to the work of the Lord. Yet despite my dedication, I still felt no power and little of God's presence.

Then came the setup for desperation! The eleven-year-old son of our dear pastor friends was killed in a tragic horse accident. We made the two-hour trip to attend his memorial service, and arrived at the church to find the pastor couple waiting for us alone inside the foyer.

"We didn't want to start the funeral until you came," she told me. "Would you please go in and raise my son from the dead?"

> *"Would you please go in and raise my son from the dead?"*

This profound request set off a cascade of desperate questions and longings in my own soul. As the four of us gathered by the open casket to pray, my bereaved friend suddenly looked up and said, "Oh, he doesn't want to come back."

Although she had come to some resolution, I was deeply shaken. It seemed I was shooting blanks in my "love gun." I couldn't even pray for a cold or a headache successfully. I wondered, *Where is the power to help those in need?* Many looked to me, hoping my prayers would help. Broken hearted for the needs of God's people, I was desperate to have the "children's bread" of healing and help for the others. Unknown to me, in this desperation God had set me up for another visitation.

A few weeks later, friends recommended we visit a church in Toronto that had been experiencing an outpouring of the Holy Spirit. I was reluctant, but decided if the Holy Spirit was showing up nearby, I certainly didn't want to miss it. So Charles and I took the plunge and attended for two days midweek.

Charles was touched by God in a tangible way, but I didn't like it at all. People were laughing, crying, falling, and behaving "foolishly." These things had happened before to me and others but had not produced lasting change or power. I desired to see an authentic life-transforming Gospel. Somewhat disgusted and disappointed (there were those *dis-* words again), I returned to the hotel to pack for home.

> **Charles was touched by God in a tangible way, but I didn't like it at all.**

As I lay in the bed that night wrestling with my disappointments, my thoughts turned to the Tabernacle of Moses in the wilderness. It was full of God's glory within, made with the finest craftsmanship and precious metals. Yet God instructed Moses that the final outer covering be made from a kind of untreated leather. The outer world only saw a dull gray or brown heap. No casual observer would ever grasp the beauty and the wonder inside as a result of the deliberately humble covering.

God's Spirit asked, "Though this looks like a big, brown heap to you, are you willing to get close enough to it to see if there is any glory inside?"

"OK," I responded, "I'll go back for one more look."

We returned to the meetings, and with courage, I stepped into the prayer line. A thirteen-year-old girl prayed for me. "More, Lord," was all she said. Simply, "More, Lord." The worship team was singing...*All of creation is longing for Your unveiling of power. Would You release Your anointing? Oh God, let this be the hour.*[2] This verbalized the longing of my heart, stirring a time of prayer and crying—nothing unusual for me.

I had come to my hurdle to leap, and I responded with willingness.

GOD HAS A BETTER PLAN

"What should we do?" "What does this mean?" These questions bounced back and forth between us as we started home. I really didn't know, but we had a nine-hour drive in which to discuss it, and by the time we pulled into our driveway, we reached a decision: nothing! We would not tell anyone where we had been. Perhaps in a few months if the revival progressed, we would send some of our leaders to investigate.

But God had a better idea! The following Sunday, after his sermon, Charles stood on the edge of the platform and asked, "Is anyone thirsty? Come for a drink!"

At that point, the normal response to an invitation to the altar at our church was about ten people (usually the same ten). But this was different! Perhaps 150 people *rushed* forward. Even more miraculous was that I rose from my seat and *joined* Charles. I had a desire to pray for the people. After all, I knew what to say: "More, Lord." All performance pressure had dissolved. This was evidence that I had experienced a miracle of personal healing and transformation.

> *At that point, the normal response to an invitation to the altar at our church was about ten people (usually the same ten). But this was different! Perhaps 150 people rushed forward.*

To my great surprise, the first person I prayed for broke into laughter, the second wept, the third fell, the fourth jumped like a pogo stick, and the fifth went into travail. Charles and I just looked at each other, and our smiles told the story. "This is it! The Holy Spirit had come in power and great joy!" He didn't even wait for us to send our leaders to Toronto.

God was brilliant to work this way. Had we mentioned a trip to a revival center, I would have likely thought the congregation had succumbed to the power of suggestion. But God came without our prompting.

Furthermore, this was a transferable anointing. I had felt nothing particularly different when the young girl prayed for me, but I could tell I was no longer shooting blanks from my love gun because when the people I prayed for finally got up off the floor their lives were *transformed*. I didn't mind that it looked like *a big brown heap of falling, laughing, crying, and unusual actions.* God was repairing pasts and commissioning people into their destinies. We had entered into a new season of Heaven on earth, resulting in God's love being sent into our families, communities, and out to the ends of the earth.

The story of the greatest revival wave of all time, the incarnation of Jesus, overflows with these same elements: diligence, desperation, and hurdles to overcome. People had diligently waited for the Promised One. The stories had been told for generations. I can imagine young girls were taught that they might be the one to carry the Messiah. These were a people faithful and diligent! They were also desperate. Four hundred years of silence, with no prophets, no savior to rescue them from Roman rule. Then the hurdle came, and oh my goodness, it was a big one. Mary pregnant? By the Holy Spirit? Who will believe that? Beyond His birth, nearly everything about Jesus' life was a hurdle of offense.

Mary, pregnant by the Holy Spirit?
Who will believe that?

Consider your God encounters. Likely they have had the same components: you have been diligent, you became desperate, a hurdle presented itself, and your heart was willing. What was key to position us in the past will likely be exactly what is needed to catch the next wave.

WHAT TO EXPECT

I have heard Bill Johnson say he has only one message. It is just 1,200 hours long. This seems to be true. We often have one major tone to our life message.

The bottom line of my message was developed while I was a midwife's assistant. Homebirths in the '70s had none of the childbirth helps available now. There were no epidurals to take away the pain, no cesarean sections, no pitocin to start or speed up labor, no sonograms to determine the gender. The homebirth process was a wilderness journey through the unknown. Forced to navigate whatever came our way, the parallels with our Christian journey are clear.

A few times, I had only moments to train a woman already in labor. I whittled my Childbirth 101 message down to one important sentence:

"The only thing you can expect is it will not be what you expected."

My *motivation* was to prevent the mother from jumping ship midcourse because she became overwhelmed and discouraged finding it was not what she anticipated.

My *encouragement* for those facing their unknown, wild journey of following Christ is the same as for the homebirth, laboring woman. The only thing you can expect is that it will not be what you expected. Then when the path is more frightening, difficult, tedious, or thrilling than we originally planned, armed in advance with this warning, we will be able to navigate the twists and turns with courage, and finish well.

SURPRISED BY PURPOSE

The uncharted journey of our Christian lives is much like a tapestry. Sometimes we are living on the messy, knotty side of it and cannot see the design on the other side. Once we pass through the snarly confusion, however, we see the beautiful picture. The passing of time can give us an entirely new understanding and a paradigm shift.

Another analogy that helps me grasp courage in a difficult time is the story of the donkey that stumbled and fell in the pit. His owner comes along to rescue it, but the task is impossible. To put it out of its misery, the farmer called upon his friends to help him bury it alive. However, every time they heaped another shovel of dirt on this little donkey, he'd just shake it off, and step up on the fallen pile of dirt. Shake it off, step up, shake it off, step up. Finally he walked out of his imprisonment on level ground. As time passed, the very thing that should have buried the donkey became his way to freedom.

> *As time passed, the very thing that should have buried the donkey became his way to freedom.*

A word from the Lord can also bring a paradigm shift. Charles and I became Christians and were married in the spring of 1972. We were like two new trees growing alongside each other.

Charles grew up spiritually faster than I did. Here we were, two trees planted beside each other, one a mighty oak, the other a little tree struggling for sunlight.

The larger he grew, the less sunlight came to me. I was shriveling up. I began praying a desperate prayer: "Lord, could you just clip back a few of his branches so that I can have some sunlight to grow?"

Years passed with no change. Charles' massive blooming increased. The bigger he got, the worse it seemed for me. After fifteen years, I complained out of my misery. "God...I think...perhaps You should just grab Your chainsaw and saw off the top half of his tree."

Out of the years of silence, God finally responded, "My dear Anne, I'm trying to grow a special fruit that only grows in the shade!"

> *God's shocking answer changed my perspective completely.*

God's shocking answer changed my perspective completely. My husband was not blocking my sunlight but rather protecting my tender fruit from the harsh elements. Even to this day, many are drawn to the tall tree of my husband and are pleasantly surprised when they stumble across a unique-tasting fruit on the tree growing nearby in the shade.

Like the donkey hit by shovel loads of dirt and the tapestry of snarled knots, what I was going through was an ultimate blessing.

More Hurdles!

More hurdles! On the day of Pentecost when the disciples *were filled with the Holy Spirit and began to speak in other tongues,* some were amazed and some perplexed, and they asked one another, "What does this mean?" Some however made fun of them and said, "They have had too much wine" (see Acts 2:12-13).

When the Holy Spirit shows up, we ask, "What does this mean?" just as we did on our drive home from Toronto. And we have an opportunity to respond to the new things we see. Some will be amazed and some perplexed and some will make fun.

When the Holy Spirit presented Mary with the opportunity to be part of the hosting of the coming Messiah, she was amazed, responding, *"Behold the handmaid of the Lord; be it unto me according to Thy word"* (Luke 1:38 KJV).

Abraham too responded with amazement when he was told his off-spring would be as numerous as the stars: He believed God, "*and it was credited to him as righteousness*" (Gal. 3:6 ISV).

But some are perplexed when the unlikely new birth is presented, like Abraham's wife Sarah who was old and well past childbearing years. Perplexed, she laughed, "*I am worn out and my master is old, will I now have this pleasure?*" (Gen. 18:12 NIV).

And Zachariah had a perplexed response as well when Gabriel appeared to him in the holy of holies saying he would have a child. "*I am an old man and my wife is well along in years*" (Luke 1:18 NIV).

In contrast, David's wife Michal responded to the unexpected in an entirely different way. She despised the new thing God was doing. She watched David dance and leap as the Ark of the Lord entered the city, and hated him because she did not understand the significance of the occasion, nor David's joy before God. As a result, she had no children to the day of her death, barren for life (see 1 Chron. 15:29).

We each have the opportunity to respond to the new possibility.

Abraham and Mary were amazed and received their babies. Sarah and Zachariah were perplexed (questioned, wondered, laughed, and doubted), but they too received their babies! The one who did not receive the promise was the one who mocked and despised.

It is wonderful if we are amazed when confronted with the new.

It is wonderful if we are amazed when confronted with the new like Mary and Abraham. Even if we are perplexed and have questions like Zachariah and Sarah, and like I did while in Toronto, God is so gracious. And even with our imperfections and perplexed uncertainties, He still sends us the promise. The only ineffective position in facing this coming revival wave is to despise what we see.

Determine Our Response in Advance

I sleep, but my heart is awake; it is the voice of my beloved! He knocks, saying, "Open for me, my sister, my love, my dove, my perfect one; for my head is covered with dew, my locks with the drops of the night." I have taken off my robe; how can I put it on again? I have washed my feet; how can I defile them? My beloved put his hand by the latch of the door, and my heart yearned for him. I arose to open for my beloved, and my hands dripped with myrrh, my fingers with liquid myrrh, on the handles of the lock. I opened for my beloved, but my beloved had turned away and was gone. My heart leaped up when he spoke. I sought him, but I could not find him; I called him, but he gave me no answer (Song of Solomon 5:2-6).

This Scripture breaks my heart. I don't want to miss any encounter. I determine in advance to remain diligent and desperate enough to listen for the latch, and arise! To hop out of bed the moment I hear the latch, and if it isn't Him, to leap that hurdle of disappointment and rise as many times as it takes! Our humble response ravishes His heart. Diligence captures Him.

I believe the Bridegroom is reaching for the latch. A wave is coming. I feel as if I have come upon a woman already in labor with only enough time for a few last-minute directives. Position yourself with diligence and desperation. Face the hurdles with humility. Hop up, be amazed, and seize the chance to go in this time with a sound of love and honor. Above all, remember: the only thing you can expect is that it will not be what you expected.

ENDNOTES

1. The Woodstock Story, http://www.woodstockstory.com; accessed January 30, 2010. See also http://en.wikipedia. org/wiki/Woodstock_Festival.

2. David Ruis, "Let Your Glory Fall"; see http://www. higherpraise.com/lyrics1/LetYourGloryFall.htm.

Chapter 11

ORIGINAL BLISS: IT'S A GIFT FROM START TO FINISH

by Winnie "CoCo" Banova

Years ago, I was reading from one of my many Bible translations when suddenly I came across the most brilliant and stunning word: *bliss.*

When I discovered that *bliss* is defined by the dictionary as "the ecstasy of salvation," I realized that this word belongs exclusively to the saints for whom Christ died![1] Provoked, I started an investigation and began compiling a list of bliss Scriptures, and every new, incredible find released explosions of joy in my heart and spirit. You see, I am not talking about a fancy little word in the dictionary or an intellectual idea. No, it is more than that. *Bliss* is a word that is used to describe *a heavenly realm that has been opened up for you and me to live in.*

THE CRUCIFIED ONE AND
HIS CROSS—OUR PORTAL TO BLISS

A fountain of joy flows from the Cross of our Lord Jesus Christ, and as we receive His gift of righteousness, we enter into His world which is *full of bliss*. It is a state of profound spiritual satisfaction that the world simply cannot fathom. Our sin has not only been forgiven, it has been taken away and its power broken.

Recently, while teaching at a conference, a woman in her late twenties approached me saying, "I am so exhausted from trying to please God; I can't do it anymore!" I looked at her and said, "You are way too young to be exhausted already!" She was crashing and burning, and had lost all of her salvation joy striving for her Father's approval. The truth of the matter is, she already had it—the Father is already pleased and fully satisfied in the giving of His Son and Christ's perfect obedience. Unfortunately, this sweet young thing had been fed a steady diet of "self effort" and "self works" from religion's all-you-can-eat buffet table. She needed to change her diet and get a good dose of the truth, which is this: the very moment that we believe, we are called to partake of His finished work. His approval and our mutual satisfaction rest *solely* on what He has already done.

> She was crashing and burning,
> and had lost all of her salvation joy striving
> for her Father's approval.

Maybe you have lost your joy too? Well, have it back again! This good news is for the youngest believer, and for those saints who have been at it for years. Christ labored and agonized so that you could be filled with bliss and joy.

BLISS IN THE SCRIPTURES—AN ONGOING INVESTIGATION

My first discovery was made in the James Moffatt translation of the Bible:

Said the Eternal to Abram, "Leave your country, leave your kindred, leave your father's house, for a land that I will show you; I will make a great nation of you and bless you and make you famous for your bliss; those who bless you, I will bless, and anyone who curses you I will curse, till all nations of the world seek bliss such as yours" (Genesis 12:1-3 MOF).

God wants to make you famous for something that He gave to you. It's true that Abraham was a wealthy man, but his fame went far beyond material goods. There was something *upon him*—it was the tangible presence of the Living God—something visible, something felt by all the senses.

ABRAHAM SAID "AMAN" TO GOD

Aman is the Hebrew word for *believe*, and it means the giving over of one's entire being into the care of another because they are trustworthy.[2] This is where we get our word, *amen*. When Abraham "amaned" God, he literally said, "Ah yes, God, You are visiting me; I give myself to You." It was in that giving of himself that he melted right into God's presence, and it was counted unto him as righteousness. Unlike wages due a worker, Abraham received an extravagant, out-of-all-proportion gift—the gift of righteousness simply because he believed the One Who Justifies. This is the foundation for bliss! (See Romans 4.)

BLISS PROVOKES!

This rich gift of bliss was not only for Abraham's enjoyment; it was also to provoke the nations to jealousy. Something is to be upon us that will provoke others to seek God (see Gen. 12:2-4.)

Because Abraham believed God, the substance began downloading right there—the famous-making bliss! Those who would bless Abraham, God would bless. Anyone who would curse him, God would curse till all the nations of the world would seek Abraham's bliss.

Generational Blessing—Bliss Is Transferable

Abraham's relationship with the Eternal One not only caused bliss to arise, it caused bliss to begin being demonstrated in human lives. The promise goes on:

> *So Sarah laughed to herself.* **"Marriage-bliss** *for a worn out creature like me, with an old husband!"* (Genesis 18:12 MOF).

Sarah called it marriage bliss! Little did she know that their bliss was about to expand beyond her wildest imagination; Abraham was to become the father of a large and powerful nation, and all the nations of the world were about to seek out his source of bliss (see Gen. 18:18). As we look down the generational line of Abraham, Isaac, and Jacob, we can see that this blessing, this bliss, is transferable and passed down through the generations. To each son, God repeated the promise that He made to Abraham, saying that He would give them and their descendants the land, the region: "All the nations of the world shall *seek bliss like your descendants.*" God Himself literally spoke blessing into each generation, and this blessing extends down to you and your descendants. This is your inheritance! (See Genesis 22:17-18; 26:2-6; 28:14.)

As we move along in the Scriptures, we see David is in on the blessing as well. In his psalms he proclaimed that God had made his line secure, that God's pact with him would never end. His bliss, his ecstasy, his joy all depended on God. (See Second Samuel 23 MOF.) A blissful heritage was his, the path of life to the full joy of His presence, the bliss of being close to Him forever. (See Psalm 16:6,11 MOF.) He also wrote,

> *Oh the bliss of him whose guilt is pardoned, and his sin forgiven!*
> *Oh the bliss of him whom the Eternal has absolved, whose spirit has*
> *made full confession! (Psalm 32:1-2 MOF)*

Have you already had your guilt pardoned? Then you have already tasted some of this bliss. It is something that you have been given already—nothing you have to achieve. The Cross of our Lord Jesus Christ has paid for it. This fact dawns on us after we have felt His presence and goodness. It is a dawning of bliss, the "wow" moment when you realize that He has already done something, and you spend the rest of your days on this earth discovering what it is that He has done for you.

This is called partaking of His finished work, which He accomplished on our behalf. Heaven says it over and over again, through the Scriptures and through the patriarchs, so that you too can believe it and enter that bliss.

YOUR SINS HAVE BEEN BURIED

That is the good news in a nutshell: we have been forgiven at a great price; we are justified because Christ was raised from the dead. It is out of all proportion to the Fall of mankind. We were all estranged from Him until that one moment when we heard the Gospel.

> *For [the Spirit which] you have now received [is] not a spirit of*
> *slavery to put you once more in bondage to fear, but you have received*
> *the Spirit of adoption [the Spirit producing sonship] in [the **bliss** of]*
> *which we cry, Abba (Father)! (Romans 8:15 AMP)*

There was a time in your life when you were not able to call the living God your Father. But the miracle that takes place in the heart and spirit and mind came at a very great price, paid in full by the Crucified One. Because you have now entered into His realm of grace, you can cry out, Abba Father!

> *There was a time in your life*
> *when you were not able to call*
> *the living God your Father.*

The Word says we have been planted together in the likeness of His death (see Rom. 6:5). And as Christ died, you died. As Christ was buried, you (whoever you were) were buried with Him. Whoa! As David looked ahead by the Spirit, He saw Christ and proclaimed that salvation had been made available. This event happened before time was even created. So when you step into the Spirit, you are stepping into a "no-time zone," the *now* of God. You can see what took place with you and Christ, how He united Himself with you in your corruption. He hung on the tree so the curse, the power of sin, would be broken over you.

When you see it, it's yours! You had to be re-created; you had to be made a new creature. Something had to be done with the old. A body was prepared for Christ to do His work; He took care of it all—His body was given as a gift to you. He said, "Here is My body; here it is—eat it. Here is My blood, drink it!"

Are you? What are you doing with His body and His blood? He said, "If you eat My flesh and drink My blood, I will remain in you, and you will remain in Me." (See John 6:56.) While I do not have five easy steps on how to eat the body of the Son of God, or drink His blood, I can tell you that reading your Bible really helps. Hunt down and search for evidence of the Crucified One. Read as many translations as you can find to help open your heart, mind, and spirit to this wonderful realm of grace and bliss that is available to you.

TAKE A BLISSOLOGY COURSE

Become a *blissologist!* Ask God to release what is already inside of you. The High Priest of the bliss is in your midst. (See Hebrews 9:11.) Wow, don't you want to get that anointing from Him, to be just like Jesus? Let Him live inside of you, be filled with the Spirit. That is what being crucified with Christ is—you no longer live, but Christ lives in you! (See Galatians 2:20.) You will say, oh my stars, when did that happen? When did I get to this point? With joy you will hear Him say, "You've been ambushed—it's a holy bliss ambush!"

BLISSOLOGY 101—WINNIE'S BLISS REPORT

Dear Reader: This is a collection of Bliss Scriptures that I've found so far. Enjoy, and may you discover many more on your own!

MOFFAT TRANSLATION

Said the Eternal to Abram, "Leave your country, leave your kindred, leave your father's house, for a land that I will show you; I will make a great nation of you and bless you and make you famous for your bliss; those who bless you, I will bless, and anyone who curses you I will curse, till all nations of the world seek bliss such as yours" (Genesis 12:1-3 MOF).

So Sarah laughed to herself. "Marriage-bliss for a worn old creature like me, with an old husband!" (Genesis 18:12 MOF)

Abraham went to escort them, and the Eternal thought, "Shall I hide from Abraham what I am going to do, seeing that Abraham is to become a large and powerful nation, and that all the nations of the world are to seek bliss like his?" (Genesis 18:17-18 MOF)

After Abraham offered Isaac, the Eternal said to him... "I will indeed make your descendants as numerous as the stars in the sky and the sand on the sea-shore; your descendants shall conquer the seats of their foes, and all nations on earth shall seek bliss like theirs—and all because you have obeyed My word" (Genesis 22:17-18 MOF).

And the Eternal said to Isaac... "I will ratify the oath I swore to your father Abraham, and I will make your descendants as numerous as the stars in the sky, and give all this region to your descendants, and all nations of the world shall seek bliss like theirs..." (Genesis 26:4 MOF).

And the Eternal said to Jacob... "I am the Eternal, the God of your ancestor Abraham and the God of Isaac; to you and to your descendants I give this land where you are lying. Your descendants shall be as numerous as the dust on the ground, you shall extend west and east and north and south, and all nations of the world shall seek bliss such as yours and your descendants" (Genesis 28:14 MOF).

God has made my line secure, His pact with me shall never end, all is in order due and sure; on Him my bliss and weal depend (2 Samuel 23:5 MOF).

Thou art what I obtain from life, O Thou Eternal, Thou Thyself art my share; fair prospects are allotted me, a blissful heritage is mine... (Psalm 16:6 MOF).

Thou will reveal the path to life, to the full joy of Thy presence, to the bliss of being close to Thee forever (Psalm 16:11 MOF).

Oh the bliss of him whose guilt is pardoned, and his sin forgiven! Oh the bliss of him whom the Eternal has absolved, whose spirit has made full confession! (Psalm 32:1-2 MOF)

Your throne shall stand for evermore; for, since Your scepter is a scepter just, since right You love and evil You abhor, so God, Your God, crowns You with bliss above Your fellow kings (Psalm 45:6-7 MOF).

Happy is he whom thus Thou choosest to dwell in Thy courts, close to Thee. Fain would we have our fill of this, Thy house, Thy sacred shrine—it's bliss! (Psalm 65:4 MOF)

But to be near God is my bliss, to shelter with the Lord; (that I may tell of all Your good works) (Psalm 73:28 MOF).

For God the Eternal is a sun and shield, favour and honour He bestows; He never denies bliss to the upright (Psalm 84:11 MOF).

Yes, the Eternal brings us bliss; our land is yielding fruit (Psalm 85:12 MOF).

Her ways are ways of tranquil ease, and all her paths are bliss (Proverbs 3:17 (said of wisdom) MOF).

The hopes of good men end in bliss (Proverbs 10:28 MOF).

I form light, and I make darkness. I bring bliss and calamity (Isaiah 45:7 MOF).

If you would only listen to My orders, you would have bliss brimming like a river (Isaiah 48:18 (said of Israel) MOF).

For you shall leave with joy, and be lead off in blissful bands (Isaiah 55:12 MOF).

They care not for what leads to bliss, their paths are void of justice; they take the crooked course, where bliss is all unknown (Isaiah 59:8 (said of violent men) MOF).

If you will turn back, O Israel, if you will turn to Me, if you will put away your idols vile and never stray from My sight, if you will swear, "As the Eternal lives!" from lives just, honest, right, then shall the nations seek their bliss through Him, and glory in Him (Jeremiah 4:1-2 MOF).

"What are these two olive branches, held by the two golden spouts that empty oil into the golden bowl?" he replied, "these are the sources of the oil of bliss, the two men who stand before the Lord of all the earth" (Zechariah 4:12-14 MOF).

Just as David himself describes the bliss of the man who has righteousness counted to him by God, apart from what he does—Blessed are they whose breaches of the Law are forgiven, whose sins are covered! Blessed is the man whose sin the Lord will not count to him. Now is the description of bliss meant for the circumcised or for the uncircumcised as well? Abraham's faith, I repeat, was counted to him as righteousness (Romans 4:6-9 MOF).

You Corinthians have your heart's desire already, have you? You have heaven's rich bliss already! (1 Corinthians 4:8 MOF).

But when Christ arrived as the high priest of the bliss that was to be, He passed through the greater and more perfect tent which no hands had made… (Hebrews 9:11 MOF).

For as the Law has a mere shadow of bliss that is to be, instead of representing the reality of that bliss… (Hebrews 10:1 MOF).

AMPLIFIED TRANSLATION

And He blessed him and said, Blessed (favored with blessings, made blissful, joyful) be Abram by God Most High, Possessor and Maker of heaven and earth (Genesis 14:19 AMP).

For the Lord God is a Sun and Shield; the Lord bestows [present] grace and favor and [future] glory (honor, splendor and heavenly bliss)!... (Psalm 84:11 AMP).

For [the Spirit which] you have now received [is] not a spirit of slavery to put you once more in bondage to fear, but you have received the Spirit of adoption [the Spirit producing sonship] in [the bliss of] which we cry, Abba (Father)! Father! (Romans 8:15 AMP).

And not only the creation, but we ourselves too, who have and enjoy the firstfruits of the [Holy] Spirit [a foretaste of the blissful things to come] groan inwardly as we wait for the redemption of our bodies [from sensuality and the grave, which will reveal] our adoption (our manifestation as God's sons) (Romans 8:23 AMP).

BARCLAY TRANSLATION

O the bliss...

O the bliss...

O the bliss...

O the bliss...

O the bliss...

O the bliss...

O the bliss...

O the bliss…Yours is the bliss, when men shall heap their insults on you and persecute you, and tell every wicked kind of lie about you for My sake (Matthew 5:3-11 BAR).

O the bliss…

O the bliss…Yours is the bliss… (Luke 6:20-22 BAR).

O the bliss of those who have broken the law and been forgiven, whose sin has been put out of sight. O the bliss of the man whose sin is not debited against him by the Lord. Does this description of bliss apply to only those who are circumcised, or also to those who are uncircumcised? (Romans 4:7-9 BAR)

WILLIAMS TRANSLATION

Now it is God Himself who has put the finishing touches on me for this change, because He has given me the Spirit as the first installment of future bliss (2 Corinthians 5:5 WIL).

FENTON TRANSLATION

…with the blessings below of dancing water, with the bliss of the breasts, and love! May the blessings of your father strengthen, with the bliss of the fertile vales (Genesis 49:25-26 FBT).

(Then to Joseph he said:) "May the Lord give bliss to his land" (Deuteronomy 33:1 FBT).

Who should mount to the hill of the Lord, to His Holy Place who should go? The clean handed and pure of heart, who incites not his mind to deceive, and who does not feast upon vice, he will receive bliss from the

Lord, and from my God win in his right. These are the kind who desire You, like Jacob who seek for Your face (Psalm 24:3-5 FBT).

The emotions of passion were stronger than I—but You can erase our sins. Happy he whom You choose and approach, He can dwell in Your Courts full of bliss; in the House of Your Holy retreat (Psalm 65:4-5 FBT).

A.S. Way Translation

When God to Zion brought us back from exile home returning, it seemed a dream, a blissful dream! (Psalm 126:1 ASW)

American Bible Union Version

...according to the glorious gospel of the blissful God (1 Timothy 1:11 ABU).

...who is the blissful and only Potentate... (1 Timothy 6:15 ABU).

Endnotes

1. "Bliss"; see http://www.thefreedictionary.com/bliss.

2. "Aman"; see http://www.studylight.org/lex/heb/view.cgi?number=0539.

Chapter 12

WHAT TO DO WHEN THERE'S TROUBLE IN THE TEMPLE

by DeAnne Clark

Call to Me and I will answer you and tell you
great and unsearchable things you do not know
(Jeremiah 33:3 NIV).

When I am sick, the first thing I do is pray and have others pray because I know that God still heals today! Why He heals some and not others, I do not know; however, I know that He can heal our bodies, our minds, and any situation in our lives. Prayer invites and assures God's response. It really does! Seeking God for answers in our own life is crucial whatever our need might be. Often we turn to others, and while we are told to carry one another's burdens, people are limited in what they can give. Nevertheless, God always will have an answer—perhaps not right away or an answer you expect, but He will answer if you call to Him. In particular, He will give you wisdom for the situation.

HEALED IN AN INSTANT

The first time I can remember God physically supernaturally healing me was in 1984, and it was incredible because I had been in so much pain with TMJ, a jaw joint disorder. Its long name was enough to scare me silly: "temporomandibular joint disorder," and it can affect the jaw's muscles, nerves, tendons, ligaments, bones, connective tissue, and the teeth. Symptoms can include a reduced ability to open or close the mouth, a clicking, popping, or grating sound when opening or closing the mouth, ear- or headache, jaw pain or tenderness, and difficulty or discomfort in eating.

I began to develop symptoms of TMJ in a time of intense stress, after my father passed away in 1984. The diagnosis was surgery; however, before receiving the treatment, I was supernaturally healed one night at a healing conference. After the teaching, a young man gave a word of knowledge, explaining that earlier that day the Lord told Him someone with TMJ would be in the service. "The Lord wants to heal you!"

I knew it was for me, jumped out of my chair, and was healed by the time I reached the front of the church! All of my pain and symptoms left, and I haven't suffered since. Praise God.

In Jesus' name, I pray for those who are suffering with TMJ. I speak to the muscles, nerves, tendons, ligaments, bones, connective tissue, and teeth and command them to be made whole and healthy. I speak to the mouth, ear, jaw, and head to be healed and pain free. *Lord, I ask for Your peace and Your healing power to be released. Amen.*

Temple Management

God is often so gracious in instantly healing us. He loves us and hates that we suffer. However, He did not always heal me in the same way as He did with my TMJ. Sometimes He chose to direct me on a path of healthier living, and would speak to me concerning my body, and the best ways to care for it. We really do need such wisdom. Our body is the temple of the Holy Spirit. God lives in you!

God created a person's body to heal itself when cared for properly. Unfortunately, most of us put things into it that are not good for it or treat it badly through lack of rest or improper nutrition. As a result, and it should come as no surprise, we get sick. God can use these times of sickness to get our attention and set us on a path to healthier living. Certainly, this has been true in my life when He has helped me to see the importance of creating an environment for my body conducive to healing and health, changing bad habits to good, and making lifestyle changes that would facilitate good health!

> *We alone are responsible for applying healthy body management to our lives.*

We alone are responsible for applying healthy body management to our lives. It takes discipline to make healthy living a habit because temporary fixes just don't work.

God has provided us with all we need here on this earth to be healthy. It is so important to choose foods that are going to nourish our body, foods that are compatible with the body, that in no way takes away from the body, but lends itself to the building up of health and maintaining life. It is important to choose foods that contain nothing that is harmful, toxic, or unuseable by the body. We do this by choosing real foods, whole foods, nature's foods, instead of refined foods, foods altered by man. Once man begins to do anything to a food it begins to lose its nutrient quality and becomes only part of the whole which is not as nature intended.

WHAT'S UP, GOD?

The first period in my life when I became sick and God chose to direct me toward healthier living was in 1995. During a time of intense spiritual warfare in our ministry, I developed a bladder infection. Never having had one before, I didn't know what it was and kept thinking I would get better. By the time I visited a doctor, it was severe. I was put on several antibiotics, which only made me feel worse. After much prayer and three months of antibiotics, all the while feeling sicker and sicker, I finally asked, "What's up, God? What are you trying to teach me?"

Within days of inquiring of the Lord, I was introduced to a book, *Prescription for Nutritional Healing* by Phyllis Balch, a nutritionist, and James Balch, a doctor.[1] I call this divine connection "God's answer." The book gave me great insight into my condition—things I should be doing for my bladder infection from a natural perspective. It also spoke of the importance of fasting. It told how fasting is a means to help the body detox from pollutants and chemicals, improve its cycle, and help it rest for a speedier recovery. Other benefits included liver, kidney, colon cleansing, blood purification, weight loss, toxin flush, clearing of the eyes and tongue, and cleansing of the breath. The book explained the benefits of three-, five-, and ten-day fasts. A three-day fast helps the body rid itself of toxins and cleanses the blood. A five-day fast begins the process of healing and rebuilding the immune system. A ten-day fast can take care of many problems before they arise and help to fight off illnesses, including common degenerative diseases.

Before being introduced to the *Prescription for Nutritional Healing,* I seldom fasted. I had always been so thin and couldn't afford to lose any weight; I also had problems with low blood sugar. However, after reading of the benefits of fasting (for instance, resting the organs, reversing the aging process, longer, healthier life), and the recommended way to incorporate a fast, I felt it was an answer from God for me at that time of my life. I began the five-day fast, and when finished, I was totally healed. All symptoms were gone, and I felt great! After my healing, it was like a light went on. I realized that when God instructed fasting a long time ago, He knew it had physical as well as spiritual benefits.

Good stuff!

Lord, I pray for those who are sick to be healed. I pray for those who desire to fast, whether three, five, or ten days, that You would give the grace needed to complete the fasting time. In Jesus' name. Amen.

WATCH FOR SIGNS

> *"That's it; I'm taking you to the emergency room."*

God chose again to set me on a path to healthier living in 2006. I had been experiencing chest pains and was very weak and tired much of the time. As always, when sick I was receiving much prayer. A few times I almost went to the emergency room thinking I might be experiencing heart problems.[2] I finally did go to the doctor, where they gave me a full exam, and scheduled a stress test to be taken in two weeks. However, before I could get to the stress test, the Lord revealed the problem.

One night around 7 o'clock, I suddenly started having chest pains and felt weak. Randy, my husband, was home at the time and said immediately with no reservation, "That's it; I'm taking you to the emergency room. No buts!"

He was scheduled early the next morning to go out of town and didn't want to leave if something terrible was wrong with me. At the ER, there were various tests. While waiting for all the results, I asked the doctor, "If it isn't my heart, then what could it be?"

"It could be anything...."

I'm sure the look on my face scared him as much as I was scared inside; my mind raced to the worst scenario, and the many tests I would have to undergo.

"...or it could be as simple as not breathing properly," he quickly added as he left the examining room.

Seven hours later, all the tests came back negative; however, the doctor wanted me to stay the night and rerun the tests the next morning twice. I declined the offer because I was exhausted and by then it was 3:00 A.M. Randy was to leave at 6:30, and I just wanted to get home.

> *I'm sure the look on my face scared him as much as I was scared inside.*

About two hours after I saw Randy off, I still felt tired and began experiencing chest pains and weakness again. I spoke with my daughter-in-law,

Tonya, on the phone and told her I was going to try to sleep. The moment my head hit the pillow, I heard a commotion at my bedroom window, as if someone was throwing something at it. I rose to investigate, and looking out, saw this cardinal just staring in at me.

"Go away!" I told it. I just wanted to sleep. It flew away, and I went back to bed, but a moment later it returned and flew into my window *again*. **Bang!**

Again I got up and told it to go away. This went on for the next ten minutes: from the bed to the window and back again. It started to weird me out because for the five years we had lived in our house, this had never happened, nor had I ever in my life seen such a thing.

What in the world is happening here? This is crazy. The timing was just too weird not to be something significant, so I began to ask God, "What are You trying to say to me?"

Suddenly, my mind replayed the emergency room scenario: "...or it could be as simple as not breathing properly."

Wow, could it really be something as simple as that?

I hopped out of bed, found the *Prescription for Nutritional Healing* book, and looked up "Breathing."

"Shallow or poor breathing can contribute to many disorders." *Oh my goodness, that's it!* It said that we need to learn how to breathe deeply from the abdomen rather than from the chest for a greater intake of oxygen which absorbs into the blood stream and through our bodies, improving cellular respiration, cell metabolism, and brain function. When we breathe shallowly, the body cannot eliminate sufficient carbon dioxide for good health.[3]

The book suggested a deep breathing exercise, which I did right away. I slowly breathed in through my nose and from my abdomen as deeply as

I could, and held my breath to the count of ten. Then I placed my tongue between my front teeth and the roof of my mouth and slowly breathed out of my mouth. Within a few minutes, all my symptoms subsided: chest pain gone, weakness gone, tiredness gone. I felt infused with energy and could hardly believe the difference by just breathing correctly for five minutes. As a result of consciously breathing right, I began to realize how shallow my breathing had been, and surprisingly, how often I held my breath. To this day, I still practice deep breathing regularly.[4]

So again, the Lord was divinely directing me to a solution. It took a little bird banging into my window for me to inquire of the Lord, "What are You trying to say to me?" And just as Jeremiah 33:3 says, He answered me!

Oh, by the way, the little red bird still bangs at my window. How amazing is this constant reminder of God's goodness and wisdom—as well as a friendly reminder to breathe properly! I call it "Birdie," and care for it as the gift of God it is! Randy and I even ordered it a special "wing and a prayer" birdhouse and mounted it outside, though Birdie does not use it. He prefers my window, I guess!

Diligently Seek

In the autumn of 2007, I was headed toward yet another discovery to healthier living. I had developed a staph infection, although at first I didn't know what was going on. Boils broke out on my neck, chest, arms, and back. As it progressed, my body weakened considerably; I was running a low grade fever and could barely climb out of bed. I had tried to boost my immune system through nutrition and detox; however, my symptoms persisted, and I went to the doctor.

*I had developed a staph infection,
although at first I didn't know
what was going on.*

He ran many blood tests, gave me a full exam, and prescribed three antibiotics, which didn't help at all. Perplexed that I felt sicker, and seeing no improvement after such a long and aggressive course of treatment, my doctor sent me to a dermatologist who optimistically suggested I wash in benzoyl peroxide to kill the bacteria.

"Really? That will work?"

"Yes, and you don't even have to finish the antibiotics you're on if you don't want to."

Wow, I was so excited. Finally after a year and a half, this infection would go away. However, after more than a week of following her suggested regime, I saw little improvement, and on the Thursday before Easter 2009, desperate, and feeling sicker, I called and told her that I was just not getting any better. So many people had been praying, I had done everything the doctors had told me to do, and Randy was about to go on a two-week trip overseas.

"Give it more time; it will take a minimum of six weeks."

Six weeks may not seem long; however, at that moment I didn't feel I could go another day, much less a month and a half. Again I called out to God to ask, "What should I do now?"

Recalling how fasting had healed my bladder infection, I decided to conduct a three-day fast. Randy supported my resolve and joined me in it. We did one day of eating raw foods followed by three days of liquids. On the final day, already feeling slightly better, I decided that

I'd continue with the fast because I wasn't feeling the need to eat and Randy was leaving for his two-week overseas trip. However, God had other plans.

That afternoon I ran across a book which our ministry finance director, Jennifer, had given me the week before, but that in my sickness, I had laid aside and forgotten. The book was *The Perricone Prescription*, written by Nicholas Perricone, MD, a professor of dermatology.[5]

Oh my goodness, it was packed with information and practical application for anyone desiring to improve his or her health and energy. Dr. Perricone's research led him to conclude that many of our sicknesses and diseases are attributed to inflammation at the cellular level. Under a microscope he found inflammation present in everything from arthritis to heart disease. Inflammation was the primary, not the secondary reason for disease and aging; as a result, he sought ways to treat, reverse, and stop the symptoms without further harming the body, eventually developing a program of various foods, supplements, skin care, and exercise regimens.

He explained that it was better to eat anti–inflammatory food choices (those with a glycemic index of 50 or less) like salmon, halibut, trout, and certain fruits and vegetables, than it was to eat destructive low-fat favorites such as bagels, breads, cereals, bananas, pasta, and pizza because they cause a spike in blood sugar and prompt the body's insulin response, which stores rather than burns fat, thus causing inflammation. Simple changes in eating could result in dramatic changes in well-being and physical appearance.

Dr. Perricone created a month-long program broken up into daily menus that could become a lifestyle menu, and a more restrictive three-day menu, designed to produce immediate results. In his book, the doctor also provides a grocery list of ingredients. If followed to the letter, and combined with exercise (a third of the book is devoted to exercise), this diet change would make a difference in the way we'd feel, and even look, with increased energy, improved memory, and an overall feeling of wellness.

I was desperate and told Randy, "This is it. I'm going on the three-day menu."

I was desperate and told Randy, "This is it."

After the first day, I felt a notable difference. Completing the third day, I felt better than I had in years, and my skin even looked better!

I knew this was an answer from God. You see, even though I had felt somewhat better after fasting, had I not begun the new lifestyle food changes, I would have just returned to my regular diet, that, although healthy, did have foods that were contributing to inflammation in my body.

What an amazing experience it was to be led on this path in this way by the Lord. Who knew that my illnesses would set me on a path of discovery of God's best for my body!

God has a plan mapped out for your life, and it includes a life of health and physical well-being, as well as spiritual. Seek the Lord's wisdom in all things. Ask Him, "What do I do now?"

Don't be surprised if a little birdie shows up at your window!

PRAYER

Lord, I thank You that You are a God who still heals today. I thank You for Your love and faithfulness. I thank You that You are always there when we call upon Your name. I thank You that You are for us, not against us. I pray for each person reading for healing and health to be hers, and I ask that You would begin to speak to and direct each one on her own journey to wellness. In Jesus' name. Amen!

ENDNOTES

1. Phyllis A. Balch, CNC, and James F. Balch, MD, *Prescription for Nutritional Healing: A Practical A-Z Reference to Drug-Free Remedies Using Vitamins, Minerals, Herbs, and Food Supplements, 4th ed.* (New York, NY: Avery Trade, 2006).

2. Chest pain can indicate a heart attack and should be taken seriously at its onset. Please seek immediate medical help. The National Institute of Health (NIH) indicates that women often experience new or different physical symptoms as long as a month or more before experiencing heart attacks. Major symptoms among women commonly reported *before* a heart attack were unusual fatigue, sleep disturbance, shortness of breath, indigestion, and anxiety. Interestingly, in the research, 43 percent of surveyed women reported no chest pain during any phase of a heart attack. Recognition of symptoms that provide early indication of onset of a heart attack is critical to forestalling or preventing heart disease. Major symptoms *during* a heart attack can include shortness of breath, weakness, unusual fatigue, cold sweat, and dizziness. Source: http://usgovinfo.about.com/cs/healthmedical/a/womensami.htm; accessed February 23, 2010.

3. *Prescription for Nutritional Healing,* 802.

4. To know if you are breathing properly, watch a baby sleeping. When a baby inhales, his or her abdomen rises; when the baby exhales, the abdomen falls.

5. Nicholas Perricone, MD, *The Perricone Prescription* (New York, NY: William Morrow 2002).

Chapter 13

To Breathe Again: The Run, the Rest, the Release

by Heidi Baker

"Go to her, over there," God instructed. I had just wrapped up preaching to a huge crowd at a conference in Toronto and was making my way to pray for the five or six thousand eager people, when the Lord showed me a bald woman laying on the floor, carried there by friends. With stage four cancer, and having lost all hope for a cure, they had pooled their finances, paid for her airfare, and got her to the meeting.

"I want you to lie down with that one dying woman, hold her in your arms, and rock her. I don't want you to get up," said the Lord.

Thousands need healing, expect prayer...

"I want you to stay with that one and just hold her and speak life into her. Hold onto courage and believe Me for the impossible; believe Me for the impossible."

"The Lord will fill and touch you," I assured the crowd as I changed course over to the sick woman, not knowing how long I'd be with her.

She smelled like death, but I pulled her into my arms and held on.

Ten, twenty, thirty minutes passed.

She was so skinny, frail, tiny...

*Forty, fifty minutes, an hour plus went by...*of hugging courage and embracing the hope of which we boast.

Months later I was attending another conference, this one in San Jose, California, with Georgian and Winnie Banov. Security for some reason was high, and they even assigned me a buffed, armed bodyguard. Somehow a woman got through a barrier and past him, grabbed my feet, screamed, and wept. "Do you remember me?"

Understand, I travel about a third of my life all over the world—if I even know what country I'm in, it's good! I didn't recognize her, but her eyes looked familiar.

"I'm the one; I'm the one!"

"Which one?"

"I'm the one. You laid on the floor with me, stage four cancer. I'm healed, I'm healed, I'm healed, I'm healed!"

Yes, Jesus! Faithful God! And friends, it gets even better. She got saved, and now leads a Muslim ministry for women full-time. She leads Muslim women to Jesus—it is the coolest thing ever!

MOVE INTO YOUR PERPETUAL SPRINGTIME

Have you been bound up in a dead, broken, or hard place? The Lord is shifting us out of a hard season and is moving us into a time of beautiful spring where we will see the flowers, smell the fragrance, and dance again with our Bridegroom King. This is a new day. Today is your new day.

> *The Lord is shifting us out of a hard season and is moving us into a time of beautiful spring where we will see the flowers, smell the fragrance, and dance again with our Bridegroom King.*

Have you been crawling, not knowing what you are doing, what you are supposed to do? Have you been in a cocoon, contemplating and even feeling as though you are dying? Are you dying? The Lord is about to bring you out into a new place where everything is freedom and spring and life and joy, a place where you can live, literally abide in a permanent springtime, in the beauty of who He is, in a place with twelve months a year of fruitfulness. (See Ezekiel 47; Revelation 22.)

The Lord spoke to me from the Book of Hebrews and showed me how the Son is the radiance of God's glory, the exact representation of His being, sustaining *all* things by His powerful Word. He makes you stable, not weak-kneed. With eyes fixed on the beauty of Jesus, you are strong in God.

For it was fitting for Him, for whom all things and by whom are all things, in bringing many sons to glory, to make the captain of their salvation perfect through sufferings (Hebrews 2:10).

Jesus *is* absolutely, supremely sufficient, the revealer and mediator of grace. So do not beat yourself up any longer because God not only loves you, He *likes* you. Do you know that? I know you love God, but do you *like* Him? As the mediator of grace, He *pours* grace over you, and when you come to Him and lie in His presence, the blood of Christ *covers* you, and everything becomes new.

SHIFT INTO MORE, MORE, MORE

Proclaim this a new day. Go ahead, declare it now. The Lord in His presence is coming into your life with His beauty and His love, and He will pull apart that cocoon *with* you. As you press to emerge, He presses to enter in, and release will come to you to fly again as a little butterfly full of His glory.

Press, push! This is a new day. Emerge from your cocoon and see that springtime has surely arrived. How wonderful that He can make you so fragile, yet beautiful, soaring and free—so delicate, yet He makes you a flame of fire where you just burn for Him as a soaring light bulb for God, as a burning, passionate lover of God.

FREE TO DANCE

"Just dance, Heidi," said the Lord recently. For someone who could not even walk or run—to be able to dance again—just the freedom of hearing those words was incredibly awesome to me. For ten years I could barely walk. Suffering from myalgic encephalopathy (ME) and multiple sclerosis (MS), my weak body hurt inside and out, and although I kept on going, it was difficult. Chronically tired and in constant pain, the Lord one day just healed me.

Although I have never been inside an actual caterpillar's cocoon, I would imagine the protective casing muffles sound. Accordingly, if you have been in a figurative cocoon, it is likely you may be missing the Lord's voice. When you emerge from the cocoon, you suddenly hear. Your ears pop open to hear the sounds of the Lord, His Word for you.

Today I'm healthy and alive, whole and full, and I dance. Dance, dance, dance!

God wants us to celebrate life, every part of life that He gives us, good or bad. He desires to take you into a deeper place of freedom where you hear the Word of the Lord, and it breaks you out of the cocoon to dance, to let her rip. It is a safe place of letting God come in and wreck us, and we are not afraid to just let go and let God. For too long, many have heard the Word and thought, *But God, I'm a cruddy person.* He wants to help you break out of the mindset of inability and incapability to one of ability and capability—and light you on fire with the Holy Spirit to finish well. You *are* free to dance, and that is a beautiful thing.

DON'T DRIFT AWAY

Every day in our ministry and lives there's crisis, crisis, crisis, but there's also glory, glory, glory!

My husband, Rolland, is dedicated to perfection, but Africa does not lend itself easily to a perfectionist personality. Weariness and stress can overtake anyone, especially when you have over ten thousand churches, over ten thousand kids, and ten thousand adults to feed every day, and a staff of 1800 people. Nothing worked properly: water not coming out of the tap nine hours a day, sporadic electricity, thousands of decisions to make, and not always making the right ones. It all caught up with Rolland.

I tried to get him to rest and relax by taking a vacation to the Congo with our friends, Anne and Charles Stock, and Winnie and Georgian Banov. But while we were away, we learned that one of our churches was attacked. Some of the people were hacked, their hands, feet and even breasts severed. It was the final proverbial straw for Rolland, who even on vacation, could not relax from anxiety.

He lost his mind; I can think of no other way to tell you. Almost suddenly, he was unable to think rationally, and dementia set in. At its peak, he did not know where he was, what country he lived in, how to put on shoes or a shirt. I'd come home at night and ask him, "Who visited you today?"

"The vacuum cleaner man."

We don't have carpets, let alone vacuums in Mozambique!

"Where are you?"

"Platypus Reef."

I mean, I did have to laugh at times...Platypus Reef?

For a time, it seemed as though we were shipwrecked on an island. Everything around began to press in. Rolland's condition worsened, and we had the needs of the ministry, church planting, children, and leadership to attend to—the mounting pressures threatened to overtake us.

> *For a time, it seemed as though*
> *we were shipwrecked on an island.*
> *Everything around began to press in.*

It was irony, really. There I was in revival, the power of God moving mightily in signs and wonders. Every week thousands of people coming to Jesus, the blind seeing, the deaf hearing, the crippled walking, another village coming to Jesus, people getting blasted by the Holy Spirit, the mission and Bible schools rocking in the Lord, while my Rolland grew worse. Tens of thousands of people around the world were praying for him, powerful healing evangelists even, yet Rolland's mind continued to waste away. Can you imagine my heart: trying to understand the miracles, the power, the glory, and those things not seeming to fall upon my husband, a third-generation missionary with a powerful, divine destiny on his life at that.

The Lord said, "Heidi, you take him everywhere; take him everywhere. Let him be in the presence even though he does not know where he is."

So I brought Rolland with me, as well as two others to help with his care, to get him washed, cleansed, fed. We traveled together until it became impossible to do so, for he drifted off into a place of complete inability to function. My heart and hope just clung to God. "Lord, I don't understand, but I just fix my eyes on You, my face on You, my gaze on You. I know that You have distributed miracles and gifts by Your Holy Spirit. Now, Lord, I do not understand, but do something here! Please do something here."

He Is Not Ashamed of You

I did not want to tell people how ill Rolland was, the nature of his illness, and how much I was hurting concerning it, but the Lord one day revealed to me, "*I am not ashamed of him....*"

For both He who sanctifies and those who are being sanctified are all of one [Father]; *for which reason* **He is not ashamed to call them brethren,** *saying: "I will declare your name to My brethren; in the midst of the assembly I will sing praise to You." And again: "I will* *put My trust in Him."And again: "Here am I* [behold] *and the children whom God has given Me"* (Hebrews 2:11-13).

Both the One who makes men holy, and those who are made holy are of the same family. Jesus is not ashamed to call them brothers. Do you know that Jesus suffered for you and died so that you could be whole and free, so that you could love Him, no matter what, because now you are no longer far off, orphaned, but part of the same family? God is not ashamed of you; it is vital you know that if you are to hear His Word and finish well.

"—I am giving Rolland rest," declared the Lord. It was rest, nothing to be ashamed of. In all of those years and years of laid-down and loving, powerful service as a missionary, my husband had never truly rested or understood what it meant to "rest" in the Lord.

HE KNOWS YOUR FRAME

As Rolland "slept," the Lord Himself ministered to those in our care; those whom we had brought home from under bridges—broken men, women, and young people—and guess what? *They* became his caregivers, daily massaging him, feeding him, dressing him, caring for his many physical needs. "It is *our joy* to love on Papa…he took us as his own, and now we take him as our own."

"It is our joy to love on Papa…he took us as his own, and now we take him as our own."

If you have a hurting child, husband, or parent, or know of someone who is in a nervous breakdown or suffers depression—if *you* are that person—God is not ashamed of them, or you. He is absolutely a loving Father who knows your frame, knows where you are, and knows what kind of suffering you are in. He is a God who is awake, alive, and able. And He will hold you in the midst of the incongruities of life, and will love and nurture you, and allow you to weep in His arms, as well as rejoice and fly and soar.

We are His children, His family. There He is, and the children God has given Him!

On that day when I meet Him face-to-face in glory, I want to bring a million children to the throne of grace and be able to say, "Here I am, here I am; I have finished well. I did not fall apart; I did not break down in the midst of suffering. I have fixed my eyes on You, and here I am, and all the children *You* have given *me*."

I will put my trust in Him, and I *will* finish well.

He Shares Your Pain

Inasmuch then as the children have partaken of flesh and blood, He Himself likewise shared in the same, that through death He might destroy him who had the power of death, that is, the devil, and release those who through fear of death were all their lifetime subject to bondage. For indeed He does not give aid to angels, but He does give aid to the seed of Abraham (Hebrews 2:14-16).

God knows *your* frame, knows *your* pain. He knows when you are doing well, and He knows when you are falling apart. He *shared* in your *humanity*. Having become flesh and blood Himself, He knows what it is to be hurting, hungry, tired, lonely, cold, naked, and needing to nurse at His mother's breast. Do you understand that Jesus left glory so that He could understand and relate to you, a flesh-and-blood child of the

Father, and show you what it is to live a life fully filled with the Holy Spirit? When you are cut, you bleed. When He was cut, He bled.

> *God knows your frame, knows your pain.*
> *He knows when you are doing well,*
> *and He knows when you are falling apart.*

> *Therefore, in all things He had to be made like His brethren, that He might be a merciful and faithful high priest in things pertaining to God, to make propitiation for the sins of the people. For in that He Himself has suffered, being tempted, He is able to aid those who are tempted* (Hebrews 2:17-18).

He understands you, so that by His death, He might destroy the one who held the power of death, the devil. *Jesus destroys the work of the devil.* As He hung on that Cross, was buried, and rose from the dead, He stomped on the head of that snake and said, "It is finished!"

The Rest, the Release

"*Therefore we must give the more earnest heed to the things we have heard, lest we drift away*" (Heb. 2:1). Pay careful attention, beloved, to what you have heard, so that you do not drift away. Some of us may grow weary in well-doing, but if we know what it is to rest in the arms of our Beloved, to hear the rhythm of His heart, to experience the run, the rest, and the release; the run, the rest, the release; the run, the rest, the release; then we will finish well.

Whatever your journey, know that in Heaven and in His Kingdom which is to come to earth, it is *finished*, so therefore push and press on for Kingdom reality in your life. Remember, as you push and press to emerge from the cocoon, He is pushing and pressing to come in. Even if things do not appear as they should, if you do not know or understand why there is shaking, breaking, or pain, focus your eyes on the prize—for because He has conquered death and the devil himself, even death has no sting.

Are You a Slave to Death?

One day while I was ministering in Pasadena, California, the doctor visited me in the hotel and said, "You need to call your family and friends to come and say good-bye to your husband, because in a few weeks he won't recognize them, and won't even be able to swallow, and he will die. This is incurable, and although we believe in miracles, you need to understand the situation." The doctor took my daughter aside and said, "Understand, your father is going to die. You need to go and see him."

"Oh God, oh God, oh God," we cried, but we were not afraid, because even death has no sting. The devil has been defeated, and we are *free* from the *fear* of death.

The fear of death enslaves many hearts, but I am fearless and not afraid to die. I have been shot at five times, stoned, threatened with knives and machetes, slammed against walls, and thrown in jail, and I tell you, beloved friends, I am a fearless little one. I am not afraid to die because *I have seen the beauty* of the realms of Jesus, and *I have proclaimed,* "Yes, Lord!"

> *I have been shot at five times,*
> *stoned, threatened with knives and machetes,*
> *slammed against walls, and thrown in jail.*

I don't want to die *just yet*, even though it is far better to be with Christ, because I still see tribe after tribe of lost and dying humanity. I will remain here for a while, and I am convinced I will live to be a hundred and twenty. Seventy more years of preaching the Gospel, that's what I have; and yes, hallelujah, I will get younger as I go! The Lord will renew my youth as an eagle.

WHEN THINGS DON'T LOOK SO GOOD

Therefore, holy brethren, partakers of the heavenly calling, consider the Apostle and High Priest of our confession, Christ Jesus, who was faithful to Him who appointed Him, as Moses also was faithful in all His house (Hebrews 3:1-2).

There I was on the conference circuit, praying for group after group to get blasted by the Holy Spirit, and I'm crying, "Help, oh God!"

> *When everything is shaking on one side and glorious on the other, what do you do?*

When everything is shaking on one side and glorious on the other, what do you do, beloved of God? What do you do when you see deaf ears hear but still have a husband who cannot even put on his own flip-flops? What do you do? Fix your eyes on Jesus. The Apostle and High Priest whom you confess is worthy of more glory than Moses (see Heb. 3:3).

One of the first people I called was one of our dearest friends, and Rolland's best friend, Mel Tari,[1] a Christian leader who has walked with us for thirty-three years. Actually, he was the best man at our wedding. Mel has seen and witnessed revival; he has seen the dead rise.

"I'm just not accepting that report. It just will not happen! I will not go and say good-bye to him. No way. No! Thank you very much, no!"

"Mel," I said, "I appreciate that, sweetie, I appreciate that...but we have prayed for *two years*. Everyone has prayed. You've prayed. You have raised the dead repeatedly, but this is what we are facing."

"It is not God's plan. I am not facing it. I'm coming to get him, and I'm taking him to Germany to a wellness center where they will pray for his healing while caring for his physical needs."

"But Mel," I replied, "we have that here. Why do I need to drag him off somewhere else? We have had hundreds of people raised from the dead. He can't even travel."

"I don't care; I'm coming to get him."

As it happened, a fellow who worked with us agreed to take him to Germany, where I would soon meet up with them. However, when I got there, Rolland was worse than before, and I thought, *Now what will we do? Thirty people are flying to Mozambique to visit Rolland as the doctor suggested, but now they all have to change their tickets to Germany?*

In my heart, I thought, *Lord, it just isn't fair; I don't think it is fair. I'm not liking this! What is going on?*

"I'm doing something," said the Lord.

"Please do it, just do it, God. I know that You are good; You are good all the time. I'm sure what You are doing is good, but I don't get it."

"I'm doing something," said the Lord.

THE RELEASE

I had to return to Mozambique and leave Rolland under Mel's watchful eye in the wellness center. Our good friends, John and Carol Arnott, Georgian and Winnie Banov, DeAnne and Randy Clark, and many others counseled me to speak to his spirit. "Speak to his spirit man. Tell it to get up and wake up," they encouraged.

So every day I would call my husband and speak, "Wake up!" into his soul.

"Wake up! Wake *up!* Wake Up! Be alive! Fly! Restore! Think! Be free! Live! Love! Feel! Wake up Rolland! It is time to awaken now! Wake up now!" Within a few months, we saw improvement as the Lord began restoring Rolland's mind, filling and occupying his house, and my sleeping man began to awaken: to remember, to care for himself, to walk, to call *me!*

Understand, here was my husband who could do nothing, who had a death sentence over him, who spent twenty-two hours a day in bed with no recall, who could not even fold a piece of paper. The simplest things were too confusing for this brilliant, brilliant man, the most brilliant person I have ever known.

And here was Jesus, the faithful Son, faithfully filling Rolland's house, my house, God's house.

Every house

is built by

Someone.

For this One has been counted worthy of more glory than Moses, inasmuch as He who built the house has more honor than the house. For every house is built by someone, but He who built all things is

God. And Moses indeed was faithful in all His house as a servant, for a testimony of those things which would be spoken afterward, but Christ as a Son over His own house, whose house we are if we hold fast the confidence and the rejoicing of the hope firm to the end (Hebrews 3:3-6).

We are God's house; me, you, and Rolland are God's house, built by God, the Builder of Everything. God wants to fill your house fully where dementia or cancer cannot stand, where anger and hatred cannot stand, where injustice cannot rule, and He promises His faithfulness over you if you hold onto courage, the hope of which you boast, *firmly,* just as I held that cancer-stricken woman to the end.

God the Holy Spirit is looking for houses for sale; He wants to occupy fully your house.

FLY AGAIN!

Rolland used to fly bush planes for our ministry to help us reach more lost and broken for Christ. Guess what? He recently passed his flying exam! Do you know what it takes to fly an aircraft? A sound mind, coherency, the ability to navigate with complicated charts, graphs, and instruments. God gave him back everything, plus, plus. God is giving back again! He is giving back what the enemy has stolen from you. Take it back; take it back! Step into a new place. Dance; rejoice; be free!

The woman with cancer danced again. Cancer is not impossible. Nothing is impossible with God. Think about those difficult, painful, hurtful things, and fix your thoughts on Christ Jesus. Ask Him to step in and possess you, that person, or that situation. Mental illness, dementia, depression: there is no shame.

Through our pain, God has healed us and has brought us closer together with our children, showing us what is important and where we needed to change things in our schedule and in our lives. As a result of Rolland's illness, all of our children and family were with us: ministering, baptizing, preaching with me. We were just in a place of incredible joy as a family and in also understanding how important we were as a *unit* to Him.

STEP INTO HIS EYES AND PUSH

Throughout this book, you have heard a lot about pushing. Today, in this springtime season, God is taking down discouragement and the feeling that nothing will ever change, and depositing courage in your heart. Courageous woman of God, it is time to rise up and fix your eyes and thoughts on the prize; push with all your might on the walls of the cocoon so that you can hear what the Lord is saying and see the glorious light of His Gospel in your situation.

It is a new day, a new day! Since the promise of entering His rest still stands, be careful that you are not found falling short of His rest. As you rise up with courage, let the Lord teach you how to lie down too, to rest and push and run and release until light breaks forth.

If you are a mother, you know what it is to give birth, what it is to carry a child, and how uncomfortable it can be to carry the gift God has placed within you. But you carry, carry, carry, nevertheless. A time comes, though, when you have to *push;* the onset of labor means *push.* You may feel like giving up. I have felt that. I just thought, *It's too hard, God! I can't do this.* **Somebody take this child out of me!** Nevertheless, as God told me, so He tells you, "You can do it. Just focus your thoughts and gaze on Me. Take courage, have courage, have faith."

It's too hard, God! I can't do this.

Once the promise is born, and you hold it in your arms, you forget the suffering and the cost; both no longer matter because there is your beloved, beautiful promise! That "child" that you love with all your heart melts your heart with joy.

God is holding *you* in His arms, His gaze *fixed* on yours, and He is saying, "Have courage, my Beautiful One, because *everything* that I purposed for you to do, I will give you the strength, tenacity, and love to do! I will give you the courage you need, and will not ask you to abort one single promise. Hold on for your marriage. Hold on for your children. Hold on for your miracle healing. Speak life into all of it. Hold on, Beloved. Fix your thoughts on My Son, Christ Jesus. Place your gaze and thoughts on Him. His eyes are full of courage, full of fire, full of freedom, full of victory, so fly, Beautiful One, fly!"

> *Oh, we step into Your eyes, Oh God, Your eyes, Your eyes. Oh Lord, we step into Your eyes, into Your house. Fill our houses, Lord.*

God says He makes His angels winds, and His servants flames of fire (see Heb. 1). Release yourself to God as a flame of burning love. God wants to light you on fire with the passion of His glorious love. He wants to burn that holy, holy fire inside of you and through you.

> *Brand us with Your love, Lord. Come and seal us with Your name written on our foreheads. Let our identity be Christ Jesus in us, You in us, the hope of glory, Christ Jesus, revealing Himself through every personality. Burn in us the love of Christ, His beauty, kindness, generosity, justice, mercy. Take us into a place where we breathe and fly again....*

ENDNOTE

1. It has been said that the greatest revival of the 20th century (Indonesian Revival) happened on the Island

of Timor, Indonesia, where Mel Tari (author of the best-selling book, *Like a Mighty Wind,* and founder of World Missions International; Mel Tari Ministries, www.worldmissioninternational.com) was born. As the Holy Spirit swept across his country, he saw the dead rise, the blind see, the cripple walk, water turn into wine, and millions come to experience the saving grace of Jesus Christ, which Mel Tari chronicled in his book. Today, he travels the world telling of the wonders of Christ, and the simplicity of the Word.

ABOUT THE AUTHORS

Sue Ahn

Sue Ahn is Holy Spirit filled and a lover of Jesus, wholly committed to pouring biblical foundations of the Kingdom of God into making disciples of the youth generation. Her passions include building strong marriages, family, and unlocking truths of identity in Christ's love to release children and women into greater Kingdom potential. She speaks naturally of the love of God in a real, down-to-earth manner with prophetic insight and wisdom.

She has been married to Che Ahn for 30+ years and resides in Southern California with him and her four adult children, Mary, Joy (husband Kuoching), Grace (husband Steve), and Gabriel. She is the co-founder of Harvest Rock Church and has been a prophetic voice for not only the local church but also in the international sphere through Harvest International Ministry.

Heidi Baker

Heidi Baker was transformed into a minister and missionary as a California teenager by the power of the Holy Spirit, and for more than thirty years has poured her life out for the poor, lost and broken in foreign lands. Now she is seeing unprecedented, fiery revival in Mozambique, Africa. For more information about Heidi's ministry you can go to www.irismin.org.

Together Heidi and Rolland care for more than 1,000 children daily and have planted over 5,000 churches!

Winnie Banova

"Joy Apostles" Georgian and Winnie Banov are a radical power team. Their exuberant, childlike praise and deep intimate worship usher in a breaker anointing for an open heaven atmosphere through which they deliver life-changing revelations and prophetic insights from the Word of God. Boldly declaring the finished work of Calvary, they minister freedom, joy, supernatural healing and wholeness by exerting the divine labor: Christ the hope of glory being fully formed in you! They also hold a special anointing for the release of creative miracles, including supernatural blessings for finances, land, and houses.

The Banovs travel extensively, holding apostolic renewal meetings and conferences worldwide. Charged with a heart of compassion for the poorest of the poor, they also host lavish evangelistic feeding crusades throughout the third world. Although the sounds, flavors, and spices of these "Kingdom celebration feasts" vary from nation to nation, they find the River of God's extravagant love is always the same—deep, passionate, all consuming, and irresistible.

DeAnne Clark

DeAnne lives in Mechanicsburg, Pennsylvania. She is the wife of Randy Clark and the mother of four: Joshua (daughter-in-law Tonya), Johannah, Josiah, Jeremiah and grandmother of one: Simeon. She and Randy planted and co-pastored the Vineyard Christian Fellowship in St. Louis, Missouri, from 1986-2001. In 1994 they founded Global Awakening, a ministry focused on training up and releasing people to affect the world through God's healing power. DeAnne's passion is to see everyone experience true intimacy with God thus experiencing and knowing God's love. As a worshiper, she longs to see everyone worship God in utter abandonment, and experience freedom in their life to be who God created them to be.

Sheri Hess

Sheri Hess pastors alongside her husband of 25 years, Dave Hess, at Christ Community Church in Camp Hill, Pennsylvania. She oversees the prophetic, prayer, and women's ministries. Encouragement and enthusiasm pour out from her life. As an equipper, teacher, and prophetic voice to this generation, she serves to see people step into their God-given destiny. Sheri and Dave have three grown children and a brand-new grandson.

Beni Johnson

Beni and Bill Johnson are the senior pastors of Bethel Church. Together they serve a growing number of churches that have partnered for revival. This apostolic network has crossed denominational lines in building relationships that enable church leaders to walk in both purity and power. Beni has a call to intercession that is an integral part of the Bethel

Church mission. She is in charge of Bethel's Prayer House, ministry teams, and the intercessors. The Lord has given her a heart for broken people of all ages. Her insight into strategies for prayer and her involvement in prayer networks have helped to bring much-needed breakthrough in Bethel's ministry. Beni's heart is to help people begin to carry joy in intercession. She believes that being an intercessor is capturing the heartbeat of Heaven and declaring or praying that into your world. It is true agreement with Heaven.

Nina Myers

Nina has had a lifelong passion to live in excellence and blessing. That life journey has included life as a pastor's wife, a registered nurse in surgical departments, a successful business owner of The Coffee Company, and most recently, the Partners Coordinator at Global Awakening. She is the mother of two wonderful children, and the lifelong wife of her husband, Max. Nina loves to set women free to be who they are, not who others have expected them to be. When you're with Nina, be prepared to laugh, cry, and be lifted up.

Anne Stock

Anne Stock is an endearing Spirit-filled combination of wise sage and wondrous child.

With disarming love, speaking from the heart of life experiences, she creates an atmosphere that brings comfort in the middle of transition and a fresh resolve and courage for the journey.

Anne and her husband Charles, married 37 years, have been the senior pastors of Life Center, Harrisburg, Pennsylvania, since 1988. They have two daughters and six grandchildren.

For more information about
upcoming conference held by Global Awakening contact:

GLOBAL AWAKENING
1451 Clark St.
Mechanicsburg, PA17055
1-866-AWAKENING(292-5364)
www.globalawakening.com

DESTINY IMAGE PUBLISHERS, INC.

*"Speaking to the Purposes of God for This Generation
and for the Generations to Come."*

VISIT OUR NEW SITE HOME AT
WWW.DESTINYIMAGE.COM

FREE SUBSCRIPTION TO DI NEWSLETTER

Receive free unpublished articles by top DI authors, exclusive

discounts, and free downloads from our best and newest books.

Visit www.destinyimage.com to subscribe.

Write to: Destiny Image
              P.O. Box 310
              Shippensburg, PA 17257-0310

Call: 1-800-722-6774

Email: orders@destinyimage.com

For a complete list of our titles or to place an order
online, visit www.destinyimage.com.

FIND US ON **FACEBOOK** OR FOLLOW US ON **TWITTER**.

www.facebook.com/destinyimage   **facebook**
www.twitter.com/destinyimage   **twitter**